# Programming Languages: C and C++

# Programming Languages: C and C++

Gracie Mckenzie

MURPHY & MOORE

www.murphy-moorepublishing.com

Murphy & Moore Publishing,
1 Rockefeller Plaza,
New York City, NY 10020, USA

ISBN: 978-1-63987-462-0

**Cataloging-in-Publication Data**

Programming languages : C and C++ / Gracie Mckenzie.
    p. cm.
Includes bibliographical references and index.
ISBN 978-1-63987-462-0
1. C (Computer program language). 2. C++ (Computer program language).
3. Programming languages (Electronic computers). I. Mckenzie, Gracie.
QA76.73.C15 P76 2022
005.133--dc23

For information on all Murphy & Moore Publications
visit our website at www.murphy-moorepublishing.com

# Contents

# Preface

C is a general purpose programming language which is closely associated with UNIX. It is a procedural language which uses top down approach in program designing. While both C and C++ are case sensitive, the latter is an object oriented language which uses bottoms up approach for program designing. C++ allows zero overhead abstractions based on hardware mappings. It also has better reusability and readability than C. It is used extensively in system softwares, video games and operating systems. This book is compiled in such a manner, that it will provide in-depth knowledge about the theory and practice of C and C++. Also included herein is a detailed explanation of the various concepts and applications of C and C++ programming languages. Coherent flow of topics, student-friendly language and extensive use of examples make this book an invaluable source of knowledge.

To facilitate a deeper understanding of the contents of this book a short introduction of every chapter is written below:

Chapter 1- The process of designing and building a computer program to perform a specific task is known as computer programming. This is an introductory chapter which will briefly introduce all the significant aspects of C programming language such as its applications and features.

Chapter 2- Data types refer to the type and method of the data entered. There are two different types of data types in C language: primary data types and derived data types. The other basic elements in C language are arrays, pointers, structures, union and enumeration, and functions. All these diverse elements of C language are thoroughly described in this chapter.

Chapter 3- C++ is a programming language that is used to create high-performance applications and gives the programmers a high level of control over system resources and memory. C and C++ programming language is an interdisciplinary subject which makes it essential to understand its related fields.

Chapter 4- There are several basic elements and features of C++ programming language such as syntax, comments, complier, variables, storage class, operator and expressions, and data types. Syntax is the set of rules which ensures that the combinations of symbols are correctly structured. All these diverse elements and features of C++ programming language have been carefully analyzed in this chapter.

Chapter 5- Some of the aspects related to C++ programming language are generic programming, metaprogramming, C++ standard library, C++ string handling. In generic programming, general algorithms are written which work with all data types. This chapter has been carefully written to provide an easy understanding of the varied facets of C++ programming language.

I owe the completion of this book to the never-ending support of my family, who supported me throughout the project.

Gracie Mckenzie

# Introduction to C Programming Language

The process of designing and building a computer program to perform a specific task is known as computer programming. This is an introductory chapter which will briefly introduce all the significant aspects of C programming language such as its applications and features.

## Computer Programming

Many computers perform operations on a very basic level like addition/subtraction of numbers etc. These basic operations are decided by the instruction set of the computer. To solve a problem using a computer, it is necessary to express the method to solve the problem using the primitive instructions of the computer. A sequence of instructions given to the computer is known as program. The method or strategy used for solving the problem is known as algorithm. With the algorithm in hand, it is possible to write the instructions necessary to implement the algorithm. Programs are developed to solve some problem. These programs can be written using some computer language like Basic, C, C++, Java etc.

### Language Levels

When computers were first developed, the only way to program them was in terms of binary numbers. These binary numbers are corresponds to machine instructions and referred to as Machine language and are stored in computer's memory. The next step in programming was the development of assembly languages. This has enabled the programmer to work with the computers on a slightly higher level. Instead of specifying the sequences of binary numbers to carry out particular tasks, the assembly language permits the programmer to use symbolic names to perform various operations. An assembler translates the assembly language program into the machine instructions i.e in binary.

Table: World of programming languages.

| High Level Languages | Ada |
| --- | --- |
|  | Modula-2 |
|  | Pascal |

| | COBOL |
|---|---|
| | FORTRAN |
| | BASIC |
| Middle Level Languages | Java |
| | C++ |
| | C |
| | FORTH |
| | Macro-assembler |
| Low level language | Assembler |

The machine language and the assembly language is popularly known as Low level language. The programmer must learn the instruction set of the particular computer system to write a program in assembly language, and the program is not portable. The program will not run on a different processor. This is because different processors have different instruction sets. As these assembly language programs are written in terms of separate instruction sets, they are machine dependent.

For writing the program once independent of the processor, it was necessary to standardize the syntax of a language. Higher-level language was introduced so that a program could be written in the language to be machine independent. That is, a program could run on any machine that supported the language with few or no changes. To execute a higher-level language, a special computer program must be developed that translates the statements of the higher-level language into a form that the computer can understand. This program is known as a compiler.

## Operating System

Operating system is program that controls the entire operations of computer system. Access to all the resource of the computer e.g. memory and input/output devices is provided through the operating system. This program looks after the file management, memory management and I/O management. It is a program that allows all other program to use the computing capability of the computer and execute them. The most popular operating systems are Windows, Linux, Unix, Mac OS X, MSDOS etc.

## Program Execution

Before writing a computer program one must be clear about the steps to be performed by the computer for processing it. To produce an effective computer program it is necessary that every instruction is written in the proper sequence. For this reason, the program must be planned before writing. An algorithm represents the logic of the program. When an algorithm is expressed in the programming language, it becomes the program.

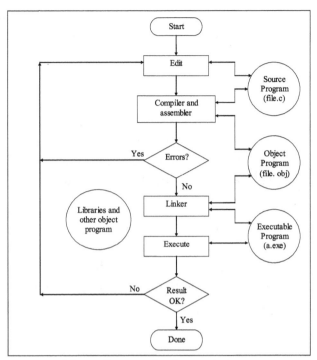

Figure: Program development stages.

A compiler is simply a program developed in a particular computer language usually a higher level language and then translates it into a form that is suitable for execution on a particular computer system. Figure indicates the different stages right form program coding to execution, Initially, the text editor will help the programmer to enter the C program and store it as file with and extension ".c". The program written by the user with the help of text editor is known as the source program. Every source program must have a valid filename e.g. "file.c". Once the source program is entered into a file then one can proceed to the compilation.

To start the compilation process, the file containing the source C program must be specified. Compiler examines each program statement present in the source programs for correct syntax and semantics of the language. If there are any mistakes or errors detected by the compiler then these are reported to the user and compilation process is terminated. The errors must be removed from the source program and then compilation process may be reinitiated.

Once all the syntax error (e.g. missing parentheses) or semantic error (e.g. variable not defined) have been removed then compiler restarts it process. Compiler takes the statements of the program and translates it into lower language. After the program has been translated into lower level language like assembly language, the next stage is to translate these assembly instructions into machine language. In many compilers, this stage is automatically executed along with the compilation process. The result of this compilation process is the generation of the object file from the given source file. This object file has an extension ".obj" and contains the object code. The filename is just same as source filename but with different extension name.

After the program is converted into object code, the linker automatically starts the process. The purpose of linker phase is to link the present file with any previously compiled file and system's library. At the end of linking the system generates a file with the same source filename but with extension ".exe". Once executable file is generated then the program is ready to execute or run. Computer system executes each program statement sequentially. If any external data is required then user must input it. Once the processing is over the result is displayed as the output of the program.

If the desired results are obtained the complete process is over else go back to the editor and check for the logical error. At this state, the built in debugger can help programmer to remove the bugs from the program. In this case the entire processor of editing, compiling, linking and executing the program. Usually, the process of editing, compilation, executing and debugging is managed under one umbrella by a single Integrated Development Environment (IDE).

## C Language

'C' is high level language and is the upgraded version of another language (Basic Combined Program Language). C language was designed at Bell laboratories in the early 1970's by Dennis Ritchie. C being popular in the modern computer world can be used in Mathematical Scientific, Engineering and Commercial applications. The most popular Operating system UNIX is written in C language. This language also has the features of low level languages and hence called as "System Programming Language".

### Features of C Language

- Simple, versatile, general purpose language.
- It has rich set of Operators.
- Program execution are fast and efficient.
- Can easily manipulates with bits, bytes and addresses.
- Varieties of data types are available.
- Separate compilation of functions is possible and such functions can be called by any C program.
- Block- structured language.
- Can be applied in System programming areas like operating systems, compilers

& Interpreters, Assembles, Text Editors, Print Spoolers, Network Drivers, Modern Programs, Data Bases, Language Interpreters, Utilities etc.

## Character Set

The character set is the fundamental raw-material for any language. Like natural languages, computer languages will also have well defined character-set, which is useful to build the programs. The C language consists of two character sets namely – source character set execution character set. Source character set is useful to construct the statements in the source program. Execution character set is employed at the time of execution of h program.

- Source character set: This type of character set includes three types of characters namely alphabets, Decimals and special symbols:

  ○ Alphabets: A to Z, a to z and Underscore (_)

  ○ Decimal digits: 0 to 9

  ○ Special symbols: + - * / ^ % = &! ( ) { } [ ] "etc.

- Execution character set: This set of characters are also called as non-graphic characters because these are invisible and cannot be printed or displayed directly. These characters will have effect only when the program being executed. These characters are represented by a back slash (\) followed by a character.

| Execution character | Meaning | Result at the time of execution |
|---|---|---|
| \ n | End of a line | Transfers the active position of cursor to the initial position of next line. |
| \ 0 (zero) | End of string | Null |
| \ t | Horizontal Tab | Transfers the active position of cursor to the next Horizontal Tab. |
| \ v | Vertical Tab | Transfers the active position of cursor to the next Vertical Tab. |
| \ f | Form feed | Transfers the active position of cursor to the next logical page. |
| \ r | Carriage return | Transfers the active position of cursor to the initial position of current line. |

## Structure of a 'C' Program

The basic components of a C program are:

- Main ()

- Pair of Braces { }

- Declarations and Statements

- User Defined Functions

Preprocessor Statements: These statements begin with # symbol. They are called pre-processor directives. These statements direct the C preprocessor to include header files and also symbolic constants in to C program. Some of the preprocessor statements are:

`#include<stdio.h>`: for the standard input/output functions

`#include<test.h>`: for file inclusion of header file Test.

`#define NULL 0`: for defining symbolic constant NULL = 0 etc.

- Global Declarations: Variables or functions whose existence is known in the main() function and other user defined functions are called global variables (or functions) and their declarations is called global declaration. This declaration should be made before main().

- main(): As the name itself indicates it is the main function of every C program. Execution of C program starts from main (). No C program is executed without main() function. It should be written in lowercase letters and should not be terminated by a semicolon. It calls other Library functions user defined functions. There must be one and only one main() function in every C program.

- Braces: Every C program uses a pair of curly braces ({,}o. The left brace indicates beginning of main() function. On the other hand, the right brace indicates end of the main() function. The braces can also be used to indicate the beginning and end of user-defined functions and compound statements.

- Declarations: It is part of C program where all the variables, arrays, functions etc., used in the C program are declared and may be initialized with their basic data types.

- Statements: These are instructions to the specific operations. They may be input-output statements, arithmetic statements, control statements and other statements. They are also including comments.

- User-defined functions: These are subprograms. Generally, a subprogram is a function, and they contain a set of statements to perform a specific task. These are written by the user; hence the name is user-defined functions. They may be written before or after the main() function.

## Data Types in 'C'

The built-in data types and their extensions is the subject of this chapter. Derived data types such as arrays, structures, union and pointers and user defined data types such as typedef and enum.

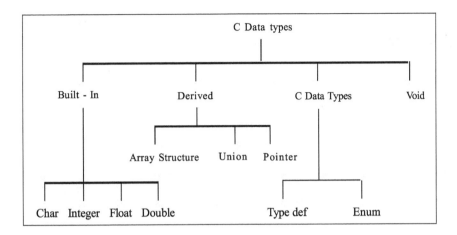

## Basic Data Types

There are four basic data types in C language. They are Integer data, character data, floating point data and double data types.

- Character data: Any character of the ASCII character set can be considered as a character data types and its maximum size can be 1 byte or 8 byte long. 'Char' is the keyword used to represent character data type in C.

- Char - A single byte size, capable of holding one character.

- Integer data: The keyword 'int' stands for the integer data type in C and its size is either 16 or 32 bits. The integer data type can again be classified as:

  ◦ Long int - Long integer with more digits.

  ◦ Short int - Short integer with fewer digits.

  ◦ Unsigned int - Unsigned integer.

  ◦ Unsigned short int – Unsigned short integer.

  ◦ Unsigned long int – Unsigned long integer.

The qualifiers like short, long, signed or unsigned can be applied to basic data types to derive new data types.

  int - An Integer with the natural size of the host machine.

- Floating point data: The numbers which are stored in floating point representation with mantissa and exponent are called floating point (real) numbers. These numbers can be declared as 'float' in C.

- float – Single – precision floating point number value.

- Double data: - Double is a keyword in C to represent double precision floating point numbers.

  double - Double – precision floating point number value.

## Data Kinds in C

Various data kinds that can be included in any C program can fall in to the following:

- Constants/Literals

- Reserve Words Keywords

- Deli meters

- Variables/Identifiers

## Constants/Literals

Constants are those, which do not change, during the execution of the program. Constants may be categorized in to:

- Numeric Constants

- Character Constants

- String Constants

## Numeric Constants

Numeric constants, as the name itself indicates, are those which consist of numerals, an optional sign and an optional period. They are further divided into two types:

- Integer Constants

- Real Constants

## Integer Constants

A whole number is an integer constant Integer constants do not have a decimal point. These are further divided into three types depending on the number systems they belong to. They are:

- Decimal integer constants.

- Octal integer constants.

- Hexadecimal integer constants.

A decimal integer constant is characterized by the following properties:

- It is a sequence of one or more digits ([0...9], the symbols of decimal number system).

- It may have an optional + or − sign. In the absence of sign, the constant is assumed to be positive.

- Commas and blank spaces are not permitted.

- It should not have a period as part of it.

Some examples of valid decimal integer constants:

456

-123

Some examples of invalid decimal integer constants:

4.56 - Decimal point is not permissible

1,23 - Commas are not permitted

An octal integer constant is characterized by the following properties:

- It is a sequence of one or more digits ([0...7], symbols of octal number system).

- It may have an optional + or − sign. In the absence of sign, the constant is assumed to be positive.

- It should start with the digit 0.

- Commas and blank spaces are not permitted.

- It should not have a period as part of it.

Some examples of valid octal integer constants:

0456

-0123

+0123

Some examples of invalid octal integer constants:

04.56 - Decimal point is not permissible

04,56 - Commas are not permitted

x34 - x is not permissible symbol

568 - 8 is not a permissible symbol

A hexadecimal integer constant is characterized by the following properties:

- It is a sequence of one or more symbols ([0...9][A....Z], the symbols of Hexadecimal number system).

- It may have an optional + or - sign. In the absence of sign, the constant is assumed to be positive.

- It should start with the symbols 0X or 0x.

- Commas and blank spaces are not permitted.

- It should not have a period as part of it.

Some examples of valid hexadecimal integer constants:

0x456

-0x123

0x56A

0XB78

Some examples of invalid hexadecimal integer constants:

0x4.56 - Decimal point is not permissible

0x4,56 - Commas are not permitted

## Real Constants

The real constants also known as floating point constants are written in two forms (i) Fractional form, (ii) Exponential form.

1. Fractional Form: The real constants in Fractional form are characterized by the following characteristics:

- Must have at least one digit.

- Must have a decimal point.

- May be positive or negative and in the absence of sign taken as positive.

- Must not contain blanks or commas in between digits.

- May be represented in exponential form, if the value is too higher or too low.

Some examples of valid real constants:

456.78

-123.56

Some examples of invalid real constants:

4.56 - Blank spaces are not permitted

4,56 - Commas are not permitted

456 - Decimal point missing

2. Exponential Form: The exponential form offers a convenient way for writing very large and small real constant. For example, 56000000.00, which can be written as 0.56 *, 108 is written as 0.56E8 or 0.56e8 in exponential form. 0.000000234, which can be written as 0.234 * 10-6 is written as 0.234E-6 or 0.234e-6 in exponential form. The letter E or e stand for exponential form.

A real constant expressed in exponential form has two parts: (i) Mantissa part, (ii) Exponent part. Mantissa is the part of the real constant to the left of E or e, and the Exponent of a real constant is to the right of E or e. Mantissa and Exponent of the above two number are shown below.

| Mantissa ↓ | Exponent ↓ | Mantissa ↓ | Exponent ↓ |
|---|---|---|---|
| 0.56 | E 8 | 0.234 | E -6 |

In the above examples, 0.56 and 0.234 are the mantissa parts of the first and second numbers, respectively, and 8 and -6 are the exponent parts of the first and second number, respectively.

The real constants in exponential form and characterized by the following characteristics:

- The mantissa must have at least one digit.

- The mantissa is followed by the letter E or e and the exponent.

- The exponent must have at least one digit and must be an integer.

- A sign for the exponent is optional.

Some examples of valid real constants:

3E4

23e-6

0.34E6

Some examples of invalid real constants:

> 23E - No digit specified for exponent.

> 23e4.5 - Exponent should not be a fraction.

> 23,4e5 - Commas are not allowed.

> 256*e8- * not allowed.

## Character Constants

Any character enclosed with in single quotes (') is called character constant. A character constant:

- May be a single alphabet, single digit or single special character placed with in single quotes.

- Has a maximum length of 1 character.

Here are some examples:

- 'C'

- 'c'

- ':'

- '*'

## String Constants

A string constant is a sequence of alphanumeric characters enclosed in double quotes whose maximum length is 255 characters.

Following are the examples of valid string constants:

- "My name is Krishna"

- "Bible"

- "Salary is 18000.00"

Following are the examples of invalid string constants:

- My name is Krishna - Character are not enclosed in double quotation marks.

- "My name is Krishna - Closing double quotation mark is missing.

- 'My name is Krishna' - Characters are not enclosed in double quotation marks.

## Reserve Words/Keywords

In C language, some words are reserved to do specific tasks intended for them and are called Keywords or Reserve words. The list reserve words are:

| auto | do | goto |
|------|------|------|
| break | double | if |
| case | else | int |
| char | extern | long |
| continue | float | register |
| default | for | return |
| short | sezeof | static |
| struct | switch | typedef |
| union | unsigned | void |
| while | const | entry |
| violate | enum | noalias |

## Delimiters

This is symbol that has syntactic meaning and has got significance. These will not specify any operation to result in a value. C language delimiters list is given below:

| Symbol | Name | Meaning |
|--------|------|---------|
| # | Hash | Pre-Processor Directive |
| , | Comma | Variable Delimiter To Separate Variable |
| : | Colon | Label Delimiter |
| ; | Semicolon | Statement Delimiter |
| ( ) | Parenthesis | Used For Expressions |
| { } | Curly Braces | Used For Blocking Of Statements |
| [ ] | Square Braces | Used Along With Arrays |

## Variables/Identifiers

These are the names of the objects, whose values can be changed during the program execution. Variables are named with description that transmits the value it holds.

[A quantity of an item, which can be change its value during the execution of program is called variable. It is also known as Identifier].

Rules for naming a variable:

- It can be of letters, digits and underscore (_).

- First letter should be a letter or an underscore, but it should not be a digit.

- Reserve words cannot be used as variable names. Example: basic, root, rate, roll-no etc are valid names.

Declaration of variables:

| Syntax | type | Variable list |
|--------|------|---------------|
| int | i, j | i, j are declared as integers. |
| float | salary | salary is declared ad floating point variable. |
| Char | sex | sex is declared as character variable. |

## Operators

An Operator is a symbol that operates on a certain data type. The data items that operators act upon are called operands. Some operators require two operands, some operators act upon only one operand. In C, operators can be classified into various categories based on their utility and action.

- Arithmetic Operators

- Relational Operators

- Logical Operator

- Assignment Operator

- Increment & Decrement Operator

- Conditional Operator

- Bitwise Operator

- Comma Operator

## Arithmetic Operators

The Arithmetic operators perform arithmetic operations. The Arithmetic operators can operate on any built in data type. Lists of arithmetic operators are:

Operator Meaning:

| | |
|---|---|
| + | Addition |
| - | Subtraction |
| * | Multiplication |
| / | Division |
| % | Modulo division |

## Relational Operators

Relational Operators are used to compare arithmetic, logical and character expressions. The Relational Operators compare their left hand side expression with their right hand side expression. Then evaluates to an integer. If the Expression is false it evaluate to "zero" (0) if the expression is true it evaluate to "one".

Operator Meaning:

| < | Less than |
|---|---|
| > | Greater than |
| <= | Less than or Equal to |
| >= | Greater than or Equal to |
| = = | Equal to |
| != | Not Equal to |

The Relational Operators are represented in the following manner:

Expression-1    Relational Operator    Expression-2

The Expression-1 will be compared with Expression -2 and depending on the relation the result will be either "TRUE" OR "FALSE".

## Logical Operators

A logical operator is used to evaluate logical and relational expressions. The logical operators act upon operands that are themselves logical expressions. There are three logical operators:

| Operators | Expression |
|---|---|
| && | Logical AND |
| \|\| | Logical OR |
| ! | Logical NOT |

- Logical AND (&&): A compound Expression is true when two expression when two expressions are true. The && is used in the following manner.

    Exp1 && Exp2

The result of a logical AND operation will be true only if both operands are true.

The results of logical operators are:

    Exp1 Op. Exp2 Result

    True && True True

    True && False False

False && False False

False && True False

Example: a = 5; b = 10; c = 15

```
        Exp1              Exp2              Result

1.  ( a< b ) && ( b < c )         => True

2.  ( a> b ) && ( b < c )         => False

3.  ( a< b ) && ( b > c )         => False

4.  ( a> b ) && ( b > c )         => False
```

- Logical OR: A compound expression is false when all expression are false otherwise the compound expression is true. The operator "||" is used as It evaluates to true if either exp-1 or exp-2 is true. The truth table of "OR" is Exp1 || Exp2.

| Exp1 | Operator | Exp2 | Result |
|-------|----------|-------|--------|
| True | \|\| | True | True |
| True | \|\| | False | True |
| False | \|\| | True | True |
| False | \|\| | False | False |

Example: a = 5; b = 10; c = 15

```
        Exp1              Exp2              Result

1.  ( a< b ) || ( b < c )         => True

2.  ( a> b ) || ( b < c )         => False

3.  ( a< b ) || ( b > c )         => False

4.  ( a> b ) || ( b > c )         => False
```

- Logical NOT: The NOT ( ! ) operator takes single expression and evaluates to true(1) if the expression is false (0) or it evaluates to false (0) if expression is true (1). The general form of the expression is:

! (Relational Expression)

The truth table of NOT:

  ○   Operator. Exp1 Result

| | |
|---|---|
| ! True False | |
| ! False True | |

Example: a = 5; b = 10; c = 15

```
1. !( a< b ) False

2. !( a> b ) True
```

## Assignment Operator

An assignment operator is used to assign a value to a variable. The most commonly used assignment operator is =. The general format for assignment operator is:

```
<Identifer> = < expression >
```

Where identifiers represent a variable and expression represents a constant, a variable or a Complex expression. If the two operands in an assignment expression are of different data types, then the value of the expression on the right will automatically be converted to the type of the identifier on the left.

Example: Suppose that I is an Integer type Variable then,

```
1. I = 3.3 3 ( Value of I )

2. I = 3.9 3 ( Value of I )

3. I = 5.74 5 ( Value of I )
```

## Multiple Assignments

```
< identifier-1 > = < identifier-2 > = - - - = < identifier-n > = <exp>;
```

Example: a,b,c are integers; j is float variable

```
1. a = b = c = 3;

2. a = j = 5.6; then a = 5 and j value will be 5.6
```

C contains the following five additional assignment operators,

```
1. += 2.-= 3. += 4. *= 5. /=
```

The assignment expression is:  `Exp1 < Operator> Exp-2`

`Ex: I = 10 (assume that)`

Expression Equivalent to Final Value of 'I'

```
I + = 5 I = I + 5 15

I - = 5 I = I - 5 10
```

```
I * = 5 I = I * 5 50

I / = 5 I = I / 5 10
```

## Increment & Decrement Operator

The increment/decrement operator act upon a Single operand and produce a new value is also called as "unary operator". The increment operator ++ adds 1 to the operand and the Decrement operator – subtracts 1 from the operand.

Syntax: `< operator >< variable name >;`

The ++ or – operator can be used in the two ways.

Example:

- ++ a; Pre-increment (or) a++ Post increment —a; PreDecrement (or) a— Post decrement.

- ++ a Immediately increments the value of a by 1.

- a ++ The value of the a will be increment by 1 after it is utilized.

Example 1: Suppose a = 5

Statements Output:

```
printf ( "a value is %d", a ); a value is 5

printf ( "a value is %d", ++ a ); a value is 6

printf ( "a value is %d ", a) ; a value is 6
```

Example 2: Suppose: a = 5

Statements Output:

```
printf ("a value is %d ", a); a value is 5

printf ("a value is %d ", a++); a value is 5

printf ("a value is %d ",a); a value is 6
```

a and a- will be act on operand by decrement value like increment operator.

## Conditional Operator (or) Ternary Operator (?)

It is called ternary because it uses three expressions. The ternary operator acts like If-Else construction.

**Syntax:** `( <Exp -1 > ? <Exp-2> : <Exp-3> );`

Expression-1 is evaluated first. If Exp-1 is true then Exp-2 is evaluated otherwise it evaluate Exp-3 will be evaluated.

Flow Chart:

```
Exp-1

Exp-2 Exp-3

Exit
```

Example:

- a = 5 ; b = 3

`( a> b ? printf ("a is larger") : printf ("b is larger"));`

Output is :a is larger.

- a = 3; b = 3

`(a> b ? printf ("a is larger") : printf ("b is larger"));`

Output is :b is larger.

## Bitwise Operator

A bitwise operator operates on each bit of data. These bitwise operator can be divided into three categories:

- The logical bitwise operators.
- The shift operators.
- The one's complement operator.

1. The logical Bitwise Operator: There are three logical bitwise operators.

Meaning Operator:

- Bitwise AND
- Bitwise OR |
- Bitwise exclusive XOR ^

Suppose b1 and b2 represent the corresponding bits with in the first and second operands, respectively.

```
B1  B2  B1 & B2  B1 | B2  B1 ^ B2

1   1   1        1       0

1   0   0        1       1

0   1   0        1       1

0   0   0        0       0
```

The operations are carried out independently on each pair of corresponding bits within the operand thus the least significant bits (i.e. the right most bits) within the two operands. Will be compared until all the bits have been compared. The results of these comparisons are:

- A Bitwise AND expression will return a 1 if both bits have a value of 1. Otherwise, it will return a value of 0.

- A Bitwise OR expression will return a 1 if one or more of the bits have a value of 1. Otherwise, it will return a value of 0.

- A Bitwise EXCLUSIVE OR expression will return a 1 if one of the bits has a value of 1 and the other has a value of 0. Otherwise, if will return a value of 0.

Example: Variable Value Binary Pattern.

```
X  5  0101

Y  2  0010

X & Y  0  0000

X | Y  7  0111

X ^ Y  7  0111
```

2. The Bitwise shift Operations: The two bitwise shift operators are Shift left (<<) and Shift right (>>). Each operator requires two operands. The first operand that represents the bit pattern to be shifted. The second is an unsigned integer that indicates the number of displacements.

Example: c = a << 3

The value in the integer a is shifted to the left by three bit position. The result is assigned to the c.

```
A = 13;  c= A<<3;

Left shit << c= 13 * 2 3 = 104;

Binary no 0000 0000 0000 1101
```

```
After left bit shift by 3 places i.e.   a<<3
```

```
0000 0000 0110 1000
```

The right −bit − shift operator ( >> ) is also a binary operator.

Example: c = a >> 2; the value of a is shifted to the right by 2 position.

```
insert 0's Right - shift >> drop off 0's
```

```
0000 0000 0000 1101
```

```
After right shift by 2 places is a>>2
```

```
0000 0000 0000 0011 c=13>>2
```

```
c= 13/4=3
```

3. Bit wise complement: The complement op. ~ switches all the bits in a binary pattern, that is all the 0's becomes 1's and all the 1's becomes 0's.

variable value Binary patter:

```
x 23 0001 0111
```

```
~x 132 1110 1000
```

## Comma Operator

A set of expressions separated by using commas is a valid construction in c language.

Example: int i, j

i= ( j = 3, j + 2 )

The first expression is j = 3 and second is j + 2. These expressions are evaluated from left to right. From the above example I = 5.

Size of operator: The operator size operator gives the size of the data type or variable in terms of bytes occupied in the memory. This operator allows a determination of the no of bytes allocated to various Data items.

Example: int i; float x; double d; char c; OUTPUT

```
Printf ("integer : %d\n", sizeof(i)); Integer : 2

Printf ("float : %d\n", sizeof(i)); Float : 4

Printf ("double : %d\n", sizeof(i)); double : 8

Printf ("char : %d\n",sizeof(i)); character : 1
```

## Expressions

An expression can be defined as collection of data object and operators that can be evaluated to lead a single new data object. A data object is a constant, variable or another data object.

Example:  a + b

```
x + y + 6.0

3.14 * r * r

( a + b ) * ( a - b)
```

The above expressions are called as arithmetic expressions because the data objects (constants and variables) are connected using arithmetic operators.

Evaluation Procedure: The evaluation of arithmetic expressions is as per the hierarchy rules governed by the C compiler. The precedence or hierarchy rules for arithmetic expressions are:

- The expression is scanned from left to right.

- While scanning the expression, the evaluation preference for the operators are:

| *, /, % | evaluated first |
|---------|-----------------|
| +, - | evaluated next |

- To overcome the above precedence rules, user has to make use of parenthesis. If parenthesis is used, the expression/ expressions with in parenthesis are evaluated first as per the above hierarchy.

## Statements

## Data Input & Output

An input/output function can be accessed from anywhere within a program simply by writing the function name followed by a list of arguments enclosed in parentheses. The arguments represent data items that are sent to the function. Some input/output Functions do not require arguments though the empty parentheses must still appear. They are:

| | Input Statements | Output Statements |
|-------------|------------------|-------------------|
| Formatted | scanf() | printf() |
| Unformatted | getchar()gets() | putchar()puts() |

## getchar()

Single characters can be entered into the computer using the C library Function `getchar()`. It returns a single character from a standard input device. The function does not require any arguments.

Syntax: `<Character variable> = getchar();`

Example: char c;

```
c = getchar();
```

## putchar()

Single characters can be displayed using function `putchar()`. It returns a single character to a standard output device. It must be expressed as an argument to the function.

Syntax: `putchar(<character variable>);`

Example: char c;

_____

```
putchar(c);
```

## gets()

The function `gets()` receives the string from the standard input device.

Syntax: `gets(<string type variable or array of char> );`

Where s is a string

The function gets accepts the string as a parameter from the keyboard, till a newline character is encountered. At end the function appends a "null" terminator and returns.

## puts()

The function `puts()` outputs the string to the standard output device.

Syntax: `puts(s);`

Where, s is a string that was real with `gets();`

Example:

```
main()

{

char line[80];

gets(line);

puts(line);

}
```

## Scanf()

`Scanf()` function can be used input the data into the memory from the standard input device. This function can be used to enter any combination of numerical Values, single characters and strings. The function returns number of data items.

Syntax: `scanf ("control strings", &arg1,&arg2,—&argn);`

Where, control string referes to a string containing certain required formatting information and `arg1, arg2—argn` are arguments that represent the individual input data items.

Example:

```
#include<stdio.h>

main ()

{

char item[20];

intpartno;

float cost;

scanf ("%s %d %f", &item, &partno, &cost);

}
```

Where, s, d, f with % are conversion characters. The conversion characters indicate the type of the corresponding data. Commonly used conversion characters from data input.

## Conversion Characters

| Characters | Meaning |
|---|---|
| %c | data item is a single character. |
| %d | data item is a decimal integer. |
| %f | data item is a floating point value. |
| %e | data item is a floating point value. |
| %g | data item is a floating point value. |
| %h | data item is a short integer. |
| %s | data item is a string. |
| %x | data item is a hexadecimal integer. |
| %o | data item is a octal interger. |

# printf()

The `printf()` function is used to print the data from the computer's memory onto a standard output device. This function can be used to output any combination of numerical values, single character and strings.

Syntax: `printf("control string", arg-1, arg-2,——arg-n );`

Where, control string is a string that contains formatted information, and `arg-1, arg-2` — are arguments that represent the output data items.

Example:

```
#include<stdio.h>

main()

{

char item[20];

intpartno;

float cost;

_____

printf ("%s %d %f", item, partno, cost);

}     (Where %s %d %f are conversion characters.)
```

## Assignment Statement

Assignment statement can be defined as the statement through which the value obtained from an expression can be stored in a variable. The general form of assignment statement is:

```
< variable name> = < arithmetic expression> ;
```

Example: sum = a + b + c;

```
tot = s1 + s2 + s3;

area = ½ * b* h;
```

# I/O Control Structure (if, If-else, for, while, do-while)

## Conditional Statements

The conditional expressions are mainly used for decision making. The following statements are used to perform the task of the conditional operations.

- If statement.

- If-else statement. Or 2 way if statement.

- Nested else-if statement.

- Nested if −else statement.

- Switch statement.

1. If statement: The if statement is used to express conditional expressions. If the given condition is true then it will execute the statements otherwise skip the statements.

The simple structure of 'if' statement is,

```
1.  If (< condtional expressione>)

statement-1;

(or)

2. If (< condtional expressione>)

{

statement-1;

statement-2;

statement-3;

..............

..............

STATEMENT-N

}
```

The expression is evaluated and if the expression is true the statements will be executed. If the expression is false the statements are skipped and execution continues with the next statements.

Example: a=20; b=10;

```
if ( a > b )

printf ("big number is %d" a);
```

2. If-else statements: The if-else statements is used to execute the either of the two statements depending upon the value of the exp. The general form is:

```
if(<exp>)

{

Statement-1;

Statement -2;

............ ..          " SET-I"

...............

Statement- n;

}

else

{

Statement1;

Statement 2;

............ .. " SET-II

...............

Statement n;

}
```

SET - I Statements will be executed if the exp is true.

SET – II Statements will be executed if the exp is false.

Example:

```
if ( a> b )

printf ("a is greater than b");

else

printf ("a is not greater than b");
```

3. Nested else-if statements: If some situations if may be desired to nest multiple if-else statements. In this situation one of several different course of action will be selected.

Syntax:

```
if ( <exp1> )

        Statement-1;
else if ( <exp2> )

        Statement-2;
else if ( <exp3> )

          Statement-3;

else

        Statement-4;
```

When a logical expression is encountered whose value is true the corresponding statements will be executed and the remainder of the nested else if statement will be bypassed. Thus control will be transferred out of the entire nest once a true condition is encountered.

The final else clause will be apply if none of the exp is true.

4. Nested if-else statement: It is possible to nest if-else statements, one within another. There are several different form that nested if-else statements can take.

The most general form of two-layer nesting is:

```
if(exp1)

                if(exp3)

             Statement-3;

                    else

             Statement-4;
else

                if(exp2)

             Statement-1;

                  else

             Statement-2;
```

One complete if-else statement will be executed if expression1 is true and another complete if-else statement will be executed if expression1 is false.

5. Switch statement: A switch statement is used to choose a statement (for a group of statement) among several alternatives. The switch statements is useful when a variable is to be compared with different constants and in case it is equal to a constant a set of statements are to be executed.

Syntax:

```
Switch (exp)

{

    case

    constant-1:

    statements1;

    case

    constant-2:

    statements2;

    ___

    ___

default:

    statement n;

}
```

Where `constant1, constanat2` − − − are either integer constants or character constants. When the switch statement is executed the exp is evaluated and control is transferred directly to the group of statement whose case label value matches the value of the exp. If none of the case label values matches to the value of the exp then the default part statements will be executed.

If none of the case labels matches to the value of the exp and the default group is not present then no action will be taken by the switch statement and control will be transferred out of the switch statement. A simple switch statement is illustrated below.

Example:

```
main ()
```

```c
{
char choice;
printf("Enter Your Color (Red - R/r, White - W/w)");
choice=getchar();
switch(choice= getchar())
{
case 'r':
case 'R':
printf ("Red");
break;
case 'w':
case 'W':
printf ("white");
break;
default :
printf ("no colour");
}
```

Example:

```c
switch(day)
{
case:
printf ("Monday");
break;
___

___

}
```

## Structure for Looping Statements

Loop statements are used to execute the statements repeatedly as long as an expression is true. When the expression becomes false then the control transferred out of the loop. There are three kinds of loops in C.

- While

- Do-While

- For

1. While statement: while loop will be executed as long as the exp is true.

Syntax:

```
while (exp)

{

statements;

}
```

The statements will be executed repeatedly as long as the exp is true. If the exp is false then the control is transferred out of the while loop.

Example:

```
int digit = 1;

While (digit <=5) FALSE

{

printf ("%d", digit); TRUE

Cond Exp

Statements; ++digit;

}
```

The while loop is top tested i.e., it evaluates the condition before executing statements in the body. Then it is called entry control loop.

2. Do-while statement: The do-while loop evaluates the condition after the execution of the statements in the body.

Syntax: do

```
Statement;

While<exp>;
```

Here also the statements will be executed as long as the exp value is true. If the expression is false the control come out of the loop.

Example:

```
-int d=1;

do

{

printf ("%d", d); FALSE

++d;

} while (d<=5); TRUE

Cond Exp

statements

exit
```

The statement with in the do-while loop will be executed at least once. So the do-while loop is called a bottom tested loop.

3. For statement: The for loop is used to executing the structure number of times. The for loop includes three expressions. First expression specifies an initial value for an index (initial value), second expression that determines whether or not the loop is continued (conditional statement) and a third expression used to modify the index (increment or decrement) of each pass. Generally for loop used when the number of passes is known in advance.

Syntax: `for (exp1;exp2;exp3)`

```
{

        Statement -1;

        Statement - 2;

        ————; FALSE

        ————;

        Statement - n; TRUE

}
```

```
exp2

        Statements;

exp3

Exit loop

exp1

start
```

- Where expression-1 is used to initialize the control variable. This expression is executed this expression is executed is only once at the time of beginning of loop.

- Where expression-2 is a logical expression. If expression-2 is true, the statements will be executed, other wise the loop will be terminated. This expression is evaluated before every execution of the statement.

- Where expression-3 is an increment or decrement expression after executing the statements, the control is transferred back to the expression-3 and updated. There are different formats available in for loop. Some of the expression of loop can be omit.

## Formate - I

```
for( ; exp2; exp3 )

Statements;
```

In this format the initialization expression (i.e., exp1) is omitted. The initial value of the variable can be assigned outside of the for loop.

Example:

```
int i = 1;

for( ; i<=10; i++ )

printf ("%d \n", i);
```

## Formate – II

```
for( ; exp2 ; )

Statements;
```

In this format the initialization and increment or decrement expression (i.e expression-1 and expression-3) are omitted. The exp-3 can be given at the statement part.

Example:

```
int i = 1;

for( ; i<=10; )

{

printf ("%d \n",i);

i++;

}
```

## Formate - III

```
for( ; ; )

Statements;
```

In this format the three expressions are omitted. The loop itself assumes the expression-2is true. So Statements will be executed infinitely.

Example:

```
int i = 1;

for ( ; i<=10; )

{

printf ("%d \n",i);

i++;

}
```

## Nested Looping Statements

Many applications require nesting of the loop statements, allowing on loop statement to be embedded with in another loop statement. Nesting can be defined as the method of embedding one control structure with in another control structure. While making control structure s to be reside one with in another, the inner and outer control structures may be of the same type or may not be of same type. But, it is essential for us to ensure that one control structure is completely embedded within another.

```
/*program to implement nesting*/

#include <stdio.h>

 main()
```

```
{

int a,b,c,

for (a=1,a< 2, a++)

{

printf ("%d",a)

for (b=1,b<=2,b++)

{

print f(%d",b)

for (c=1,c<=2,c++)

{

print f( " My Name is Sunny \n");

                                          }

                          }

                  }

}
```

## Multi Branching Statement (Switch), Break, and Continue

For effective handling of the loop structures, C allows the following types of control break statements.

- Break Statement
- Continue Statement

## Break Statement

The break statement is used to terminate the control form the loops or to exit from a switch. It can be used within a for, while, do-while, for.

The general format is:

```
break;
```

If break statement is included in a while, do-while or for then control will immediately be transferred out of the loop when the break statement is encountered.

Example:

```
for ( ; ; ) normal loop

{

break

Condition

within loop

scanf ("%d",&n);

if ( n < -1)

break;

sum = sum + n;

}
```

## The Continue Statement

The continue statement is used to bypass the remainder of the current pass through a loop. The loop does not terminate when a continue statement is encountered. Rather, the remaining loop statements are skipped and the proceeds directly to the next pass through the loop. The "continue" that can be included with in a while a do-while and a for loop statement.

General form:

```
continue;
```

The continue statement is used for the inverse operation of the break statement.

```
Condition

with in loop

Remaining part of loop

continue
```

Example:

```
while (x<=100)

{
```

```
if (x <= 0)

{

printf ("zero or negative value found \n");

continue;

}

}
```

The above program segment will process only the positive whenever a zero or negative value is encountered, the message will be displayed and it continue the same loop as long as the given condition is satisfied.

## Differences between Break and Continue

| Break | Continue |
|---|---|
| Break is a key word used to terminate the loop or exit from the block. The control jumps to next statement after the loop or block. | Continue is a keyword used for containing the next iteration of the loop. |
| Break statements can be used with for, while, do-while, and switch statement. When break is used in nested loops, then only the innermost loop is terminated. | This statement when occurs in a loop does not terminate it rather skips the statements after this continue statement and the control goes for next iteration. 'Continue' can be used with for, while and do- while loop. |
| Syntax:{ statement1; statement2; statement3; break;} | Syntax: { statement1; continue; statement2; statement3; break; } |
| Example :Switch ( choice){ Case 'y': printf("yes"); break; Case 'n':printf("NO"); break;} | Example:- I = 1, j=0;While( i<= 7){ I = I + 1; If(( I = = 6) Continue; j = j + 1;} |
| When the case matches with the choice entered, the corresponding case block gets executed. When 'break' statement is executed, the control jumps out of the switch statement. | In the above loop, when value of ' i becomes 6' continue statement is executed. So, j= j+1 is skipped and control is transferred to beginning of while loop. |

## Unconditional Branching (go to statement)

### go to statement

The go to statement is used to alter the program execution sequence by transferring the control to some other part of the program.

### Syntax

Where label is an identifier used to label the target statement to which the control would be transferred the target statement.

**Syntax:**

```
goto<label>;

label :

statements;
```

**Example:**

```
#include <stdio.h>

main();

{

inta,b;

printf ("Enter the two numbers");

scanf ("%d %d",&a,&b);

if (a>b)

gotobig;

else

gotosmall;

big :printf ("big value is %d",a);

gotostop;

small :printf ("small value is %d",b);

gotostop;

stop;

}
```

# Features of C

C is a general-purpose high level language that was originally developed for the UNIX operating system. The UNIX operating system and virtually all UNIX applications are written in C language. C has now become a widely used professional language for various reasons. Figure indicates feature of c at a glance.

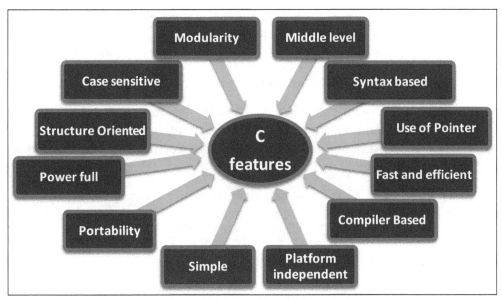

Figure: Features of C – at a glance.

It is a very simple and easy language. C language is mainly used for develop desktop based application. All other programming languages were derived directly or indirectly from C programming concepts. C language has following features:

- Simple: Every c program can be written in simple English language so that it is very easy to understand and developed by programmer.

- Portability: C programs are portable. It is the concept of carrying the instruction from one system to another system. In C language .C file contain source code, we can edit also this code. .exe file contain application, only we can execute this file. When we write and compile any C program on window operating system that program easily run on other window based system.

- Powerful: C is a very powerful programming language, it have a wide verity of data types, functions, control statements, decision making statements, etc.

- Structure oriented: C is a Structure oriented programming language.Structure oriented programming language aimed on clarity of program, reduce the complexity of code, using this approach code is divided into sub-program/subroutines. These programming have rich control structure.

- Case sensitive: It is a case sensitive programming language. In C programming 'break and BREAK' both are different.

- Modularity: It is concept of designing an application in subprogram that is procedure oriented approach. In c programming we can break our code in subprogram. For example we can write a calculator programs in C language with divide our code in subprograms.

- Middle level language: C programming language can supports two level programming instructions with the combination of low level and high level language that's why it is called middle level programming language.

- Syntax based language: C is a strongly tight syntax based programming language.

- Efficient use of pointers: Pointers is a variable which hold the address of another variable, pointer directly direct access to memory address of any variable due to this performance of application is improve. In C language also concept of pointer are available.

- Fast and Efficient: C programs are fast to compile and run efficiently.

- Compiler based C is a compiler based programming language that means without compilation no C program can be executed. First we need compiler to compile our program and then execute.

- Platform independent: A language is said to be platform independent when the program executes independent of the computer hardware and operating system.

## Applications of C

The applications of C are not only limited to the development of operating systems, like Windows or Linux, but also in the development of GUIs (Graphical User Interfaces) and, IDEs (Integrated Development Environments). Here are some striking applications offered by the C programming language:

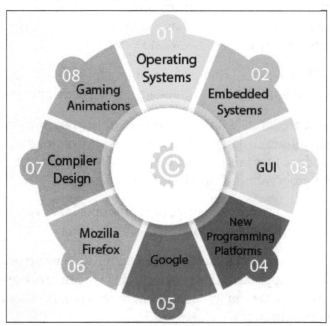

- Operating Systems: The first operating system to be developed using a high-level programming language was UNIX, which was designed in the C programming language. Later on, Microsoft Windows and various Android applications were scripted in C.

- Embedded Systems: The C programming language is considered an optimum choice when it comes to scripting applications and drivers of embedded systems, as it is closely related to machine hardware.

- GUI: GUI stands for Graphical User Interface. Adobe Photoshop, one of the most popularly used photo editors since olden times, was created with the help of C. Later on, Adobe Premiere and Illustrator were also created using C.

- New Programming Platforms: Not only has C given birth to C++, a programming language including all the features of C in addition to the concept of object-oriented programming but, various other programming languages that are extensively used in today's world like MATLAB and Mathematica. It facilitates the faster computation of programs.

- Google: Google file system and Google chromium browser were developed using C/C++. Not only this, the Google Open Source community has a large number of projects being handled using C/C++.

- Mozilla Firefox and Thunderbird: Since Mozilla Firefox and Thunderbird were open-source email client projects, they were written in C/C++.

- MySQL: MySQL, again being an open-source project, used in Database Management Systems was written in C/C++.

- Compiler Design: One of the most popular uses of the C language was the creation of compilers. Compilers for several other programming languages were designed keeping in mind the association of C with low-level languages, making it easier to be comprehensible by the machine. Several popular compilers were designed using C such as Bloodshed Dev-C, Clang C, MINGW, and Apple C.

- Gaming and Animation: Since the C programming language is relatively faster than Java or Python, as it is compiler-based, it finds several applications in the gaming sector. Some of the most simple games are coded in C such as Tic-Tac-Toe, The Dino game, The Snake game and many more. Increasing advanced versions of graphics and functions, Doom3 a first-person horror shooter game was designed by id Software for Microsoft Windows using C in 2004.

# Elements in C Language

Data types refer to the type and method of the data entered. There are two different types of data types in C language: primary data types and derived data types. The other basic elements in C language are arrays, pointers, structures, union and enumeration, and functions. All these diverse elements of C language are thoroughly described in this chapter.

## Data Types

Every C program basically has five main parts: preprocessor commands, functions, variables, statements & expressions and comments. In this module, we shall understand several aspects of C languages related to character set, tokens, identifiers, keywords, variables and constants.

Before we receive the input, it is necessary to have a place to store that input. In programming language, input and data are stored in variables. There are several types of variables. One needs to declare a variable to tell the compiler about the data type and the name of the variable. Several basic types like int, float, char are present in C language. A variable of type int stores integers i.e. numbers without decimal point, a variable type float stores numbers with decimal places and a variable type char stores a single character.

### Character Set of C

While writing any program in C one needs to use different statements. Every C program is a set of statements and each statement is made out of some valid characters allowed by the language. A character denotes any alphabet, digit or special symbols used to represent information. The character set is the fundamental element of any programming language and they are used to represent information.

Like any natural language, C programming language also have well defined character set, which is useful to design any program. C does neither use nor does it requires the use of every character found on a modern computer keyboard.

Table: Character Set of C.

| Types | Character Set |
|---|---|
| Lowercase letters | a to z |

| Uppercase letters | A to Z |
|---|---|
| Digits | 0 to 9 |
| Special characters | + - * / \ ! @ # $ & ( ) { } |
| White spaces | Tab or newline or space |

Table: Special characters in C.

| Symbol | Meaning | Symbol | Meaning |
|---|---|---|---|
| ~ | Tilde | ! | Exclamation mark |
| # | Number sign | $ | Dollar sign |
| % | Percent sign | ^ | Caret |
| & | Ampersand | * | Asterisk |
| ( | Left parenthesis | ) | Right parenthesis |
| _ | Underscore | + | Plus sign |
| = | Equal to sign | \| | Vertical bar |
| \ | Backslash | ' | Apostrophe |
| - | Minus sign | " | Quotation mark |
| { | Left brace | } | Right brace |
| [ | Left bracket | ] | Right bracket |
| < | Opening angle bracket | > | Closing angle bracket |
| : | Colon | ; | Semicolon |
| . | Period | / | Slash |

## C Tokens

After learning the character set of C language, it will be easy to understand the other building blocks of C programming language. In any language, the individual words and punctuation marks are called tokens or lexical units. In a C source program, the smallest individual unit recognized by the compiler is the "token". Figure indicates the classification of tokens.

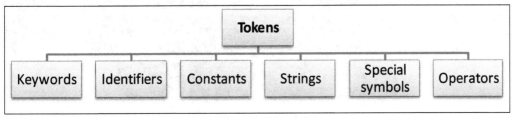

Figure: Classification of Tokens.

C tokens are the basic building blocks in C language which are constructed together to write a C program. Table indicates different tokens along with their meaning.

Table: Types of C Tokens.

| Token | Meaning | Example |
|---|---|---|
| Keyword | A set of reserved words with meaningful names. | int, float, for, while |
| Identifier | Term normally used for variables. | main, a, b |
| Constants | Fixed values assigned to variable. | 5, 10 |
| Strings | Sequence of characters. | "Hello" |
| Special symbols | Symbol representing characters other than alphabets and digits. | (,),{,} |
| Operators | Mathematical or nonmathematical symbol. | +,-,*,/, ++ |

## Keywords

In c language, programs are written from a set of reserved words. C keeps a small set of keywords for its own use. Keywords have standard and predefined meaning in C language. C keywords are the words that convey special meaning to the C compiler. These words provide control and perform special function with the help of libraries supported by compiler.

Each keyword is meant to perform a specific function in a C program. These keywords cannot be used as identifiers or variable name in the program. This is a common restriction with programming languages hence these are also called as reserved words. Keywords are not written in upper-case letters. Figure shows the list of keywords used in Standard C language.

| Auto | break | case | char | const | continue | default |
|---|---|---|---|---|---|---|
| do | double | else | enum | extern | float | for |
| goto | if | int | long | register | return | short |
| signed | sizeof | static | struct | switch | typedf | union |
| | unsigned | void | volatile | while | | |

Figure: C keywords.

All keywords must be written in lower case. There are at least 32 keywords available in C. These keywords are grouped in ten different categories based on their purpose as shown in table.

Table: Classification of Keywords.

|      | Type            | Example                           |
|------|-----------------|-----------------------------------|
| 1.   | Data types      | int, float, char, double          |
| 2.   | Qualifiers      | signed, unsigned, short, long     |
| 3.   | User defined    | typedef, enum                     |
| 4.   | Storage classes | auto, extern, register, static    |
| 5.   | Loop            | for, while, do                    |
| 6.   | Decision        | if, else, switch, case, default   |
| 7.   | Jump            | goto, continue, break             |
| 8    | Function        | void, return                      |
| 9.   | Derived         | struct , union                    |
| 10.  | Others          | const, volatile, sizeof           |

## Identifiers

Each basic element of C program is given a name called identifier. Names are given to identify variables, functions and arrays. Every data object needs some storage space in the computer memory. To refer these locations we use references, known as identifiers. Rules for naming the identifier are:

- First character of identifier should be an alphabet or underscore.

- Identifiers can use a-z, A-Z, and 0-9 as succeeding characters.

- Punctuation and special characters are not allowed except underscore.

- Identifiers may be 31 to 40 characters long.

- Identifier should not be a keyword.

Example:

```
Valid identifiers are - temp, average, net_salary etc.
```

## Constants

C allows you to declare constants. Constants refer to the data that do not change their values during the program execution. A constant is a number, character or character string that can be used as a value in program. Constants may be belonging to any of the data types. You can declare a constant, like a variable declaration but its value cannot be changed. The const keyword is to declare a constant, as shown below:

Syntax:

```
const data_type variable_name=value;
```

Example:

```
const float p = 190.5;

const int a =23;
```

We can declare the const before or after the type. Choose any one out of it. It is usual to initialize a const with a value because it cannot get a value using any other way. The preprocessor #define can also be used to define constants in a program. For example, #define k = 113;

## Types of C constants

| Integer constants | (e.g. 5, -23 etc.) |
|---|---|
| Floating point constants | (e.g. 3.14, 1.6213 etc.) |
| Octal & Hexadecimal constants | (e.g. O43, O61, ox2f etc.) |
| Character constants | (e.g. „p", "e" etc.) |
| String constants | (e.g. "Sum", "Root" etc.) |
| Backlash character constants | (e.g. \t, \n etc.) |

## Variables

In every c program, all variables must be declared before their usage. Every variable has a name and a value. A memory location is used to store the value of the variable. Variable is a name given to memory location where a program can store the actual data. As the name indicates the value of variable may change during the program execution. Variables may use any of the data types like int, float, char etc to identify the type of value stored. Variable is one of the basic building blocks of c program which is also called as identifier. The general form of variable declaration is:

```
data_type variable_list;
```

Examples:

```
int i,j,k;

float a, b, sum;
```

Variables are initialized with an equal sign followed by a constant expression. Variables may be initialized in their declaration. The general form of declarations is:

```
variable_name = value;
```

or

```
data_type variable_name=value;
```

Examples:

```
i= 1;

int count =0;
```

## Rules for Naming Variables

- Variable names must begin with letter of alphabet. The first character of a C variable cannot begin with a digit.

- It is legal to start a variable name with underscore character but this is discouraged.

- Subsequent characters may consist of any combination of alphabets, digits and underscores.

- Variable name cannot be a reserved keyword.

- No special characters are permitted in the variable name.

- Blank spaces are not allowed.

- Variable name should not be more than thirty-one (31) characters.

- Before a variable name can be used in computation, it must be assigned a value.

It is conventional to avoid the use of capital letters in variable names. These are used for names of constants. Some old implementations of C only use the first 8 characters of a variable name. Most modern ones don't apply this limit though. The rules governing variable names also apply to the names of functions. There are three types of variables in C language to specify the scope of the variable. These are shown in table.

Table: Types of variables.

| Types of variable | Scope |
|---|---|
| Local variables | • Scope of local variables will be within the function.<br>• These variables cannot be accessed outside the function |
| Global variables | • Scope of global variables will be throughout the program. Variables can be accessed anywhere in the program.<br>• These variables are defined outside the main function so that these are visible to other functions. |
| Environment variable | • These variables will be available for all C programs and applications.<br>• These variables can be accessed from anywhere in C program without declaring and initializing in the program. |

Data types specify how and what type of data is to be entered into the program. C data types are defined as the data storage format that a variable can store a data to perform a specific operation. Data types are used to define a variable before its use in a program.

C language has some predefined set of data types to handle various kinds of data that is normally used in our program. Data types define a system for declaring variables and functions of different types. These data types have different storage capacities. The type of a variable defines how much storage space it occupies. There are four data types in C language as shown in Table.

Table: C data types.

| | Types | Data Types |
|---|---|---|
| 1 | Basic data types | int, char, float, double |
| 2 | Enumeration data type | Enum |
| 3 | Derived data type | pointer, array, structure, union |
| 4 | Void data type | Void |

## Basic Data Types

These data types are basically defined for arithmetic type of data. There are four types: integer type, floating point type, double precision type and character type.

## Integer Data Type

Integer data type allows a variable to store numeric values. "int" keyword is used to define integer numbers. Table below provides different standard data types. It also includes storage sizes and range of possible values.

Table: Standard integer types.

| Type | Storage size | Value range |
|---|---|---|
| int | 2 or 4 bytes | -32,768 to 32,767 or -2,147,483,648 to 2,147,483,647 |
| unsigned int | 2 or 4 bytes | 0 to 65,535 or 0 to 4,294,967,295 |
| short | 2 bytes | -32,768 to 32,767 |
| unsigned short | 2 bytes | 0 to 65,535 |
| long | 4 bytes | -2,147,483,648 to 2,147,483,647 |
| unsigned long | 4 bytes | 0 to 4,294,967,295 |

## Type Specifiers

There are 5 different types" specifiers – short, long, long long, signed, and unsigned. For example, if the specifier long is placed before int declaration, the declared integer variable range is extended on some computers i.e. in place of 16-bits integer value it can have 32 bits. Table -7 give the details of these data types. The amount of memory space to be allocated for a variable is derived by modifiers. Modifiers are prefixed with basic data types to modify (either increase or decrease) the amount of storage space allocated to a variable. For example, storage space for int data type is 4 byte for 32 bit processor. We can increase the range by using long int which is 8 byte. We can decrease the range by using short int which is 2 byte.

int is used to define integer numbers. For example:

```
int a=15;
```

This statement declares 'a' as integer variable and assigns an integer value to it.

```
{

int Count;

Count = 5;

}
```

## Floating Data Type

Floating type variables can hold real numbers such as 5.49, -2.73 etc. Usually keywords float or double can be used for declaring floating type variable. For example:

```
float x1;

double x2;
```

Here x1 and x2 are floating type variables. Float data type allows a variable to store decimal values. Storage size of float data type is 4. This also varies depend upon the processor in the CPU as "int" data type. In float data type, we can use up-to 6 digits after decimal. For example, 21.123456 can be stored in a variable using float data type. Double data type is also same as float data type which allows up-to 10 digits after decimal. Following table gives you details about standard floating-point types with storage sizes and value ranges and their precision:

Table: Floating point types.

| Type | Storage size | Value range | Precision |
|------|------------|-------------|-----------|
| float | 4 byte | 1E-38 to 3.4E+38 | 6 decimal places |
| double | 8 byte | 2.3E-308 to 1.7E+308 | 15 decimal places |
| long double | 10 byte | 3.4E-4932 to 1.1E+4932 | 19 decimal places |

The header file float.h defines macros that allow you to use these values and other details about the binary representation of real numbers in the programs.

## Character Data Type

To declare a variable of type character, a keyword char is used. This data type allows a variable to store only one character. For example:

```
char c;
```

To assign or store a character value in a char data type should be declared. A value „A" can be stored using char data type using following statement:

```
c="A";
```

One can assign or store a single character in char variable. To store more than one character, please refer to C-strings in the later modules. Table shows different character types along with storage sizes and range.

Table: Char types.

| Type | Storage size | Value range |
|---|---|---|
| char | 1 byte | -128 to 127 or 0 to 255 |
| unsigned char | 1 byte | 0 to 255 |
| signed char | 1 byte | -128 to 127 |

```
{

char Letter;

Letter = 'x';

}
```

## Enumeration Data Type In C

Enumeration data type allows user to define their own data type. Keyword enum is used to define enumerated data type. Enumeration data type basically defines a set of named integers. A variable with enumeration type stores one of the values of the enumeration set defined by that type. Enumeration data type consists of named integer constants as a list. It start with 0 (zero) by default and value is incremented by 1 for the sequential identifiers in the list. Let us consider general syntax Enum syntax in C:

```
enum identifier {value1, value2,.....value n};
```

Here enum is the keword defining identifier as the user defined variable of enumeration data type and different values are allotted for identifier are defined. Let us take an example:

```
enum month { Jan, Feb, Mar }; or
```

```
/* Jan, Feb and Mar variables will be assigned to 0, 1 and 2 respec-
tively by default */ enum month { Jan = 1, Feb, Mar };
```

```
/* Feb and Mar variables will be assigned to 2 and 3 respectively by
default */ enum month { Jan = 20, Feb, Mar };
```

```
/* Jan is assigned to 20. Feb and Mar variables will be assigned to 21
and 22 respectively by default */
```

The above enum functionality can also be implemented by "#define" preprocessor directive as given below. Above enum example is same as given below:

```
#define Jan 20;
```

```
#define Feb 21;
```

```
#define Mar 22;
```

C – enum example program:

```
#include <stdio.h>

int main()

{

enum Month { Jan = 0, Feb, Mar };

enum Month month = Mar;

if(month == 0)

printf("Value of Jan");

else if(month == 1)

printf("Month is Feb");

if(month == 2)

printf("Month is Mar");

}
```

Output: Month is Mar.

## The Void Type

The main reason for void is to declare a function that has no return value. The term void is used in the sense of empty rather that invalid. All c functions are considered as the integer type unless specified. Void is an empty data type that has no value. This can be used in functions and pointers. Table indicates three kinds of methods to use void data type.

Table: Utility of void function.

| Type | Description | Example |
|------|-------------|---------|
| Function returns as void | Function which do not return any value. | void termin( int status); |
| Function arguments as void | Function which do not accept any parameter. | int conver(void); |
| Pointers to void | A pointer of type void * represent the address of an object. | Void *fetch(bsize size); |

## Derived Type

The basic data types studied so far are primitive data types where the type is not defined in terms of other data types. The derived data types are those that are defined in terms of other data types. Derived data types are made of simpler data types and made of integers or characters or strings etc. There are five derived data types as shown below:

- Array types
- Pointer types
- Structure types
- Union types
- Function types

## Arrays

An array is a systematic arrangement of similar objects, usually in rows and columns. An array stores a fixed-size sequential collection of elements of the same type. An array is used to store a collection of data, but it is often more useful to think of an array as a collection of variables of the same type.

In C language, it is possible to assign a single name to whole group of similar data. Let us consider an example of group of students whose marks are to be recorded. Let us assign a common name say x to all the data. Each element in the array can be assessed by its position within the list of items as shown in figure.

Table :(a) List of items, (b) List items with subscripted variable (c) Array representation.

| x | | |
|---|---|---|
| (a) | (b) | (c) |
| 55 | $X_1$=55 | x[1]=55 |
| 95 | $X_2$=95 | x[2]=95 |
| 64 | $X_3$=64 | x[3]=64 |
| 79 | $X_4$=79 | x[4]=79 |
| 63 | $X_5$=63 | x[5]=63 |

In mathematics, a subscript is a number written to the right of variable name, slightly below the line, usually small in font. Subscript indicates the position of a particular element with respect to the rest of elements. As it is impossible to display subscripted numbers on the standard computer, the numbers are enclosed in parentheses. A subscript is also known as index. In C language subscript starts at'o' rather than '1' and cannot be negative.

- Array is a collection of variables belongings to the same data type. The group of data of same data type can store in an array.

- An array is a collection of same type of elements which are sheltered under a common name.

An array can be visualized as a row in a table, whose each successive block can be thought of as memory bytes containing one element.

Table: Array of five elements

| Element 1 | Element 2 | Element 3 | Element 4 | Element 5 |
|---|---|---|---|---|

An array has following properties:

- Type: Data type of array elements.

- Location: Location of first element of the array.

- Length: Number of data elements in the array.

- Size: Length of the array times the size of an element.

These arrays are also called as linear or one-dimensional array. The number of 8 bits-bytes that each element occupies depends on the type of array. If type of array is 'char' then it means the array stores character elements. Since each character occupies one byte so elements of a character array occupy one byte each.

- Array belongs to any of the data types.

- Array size must be a constant value.

- Always, continuous (adjacent) memory locations are used to store array elements in memory.

- It is a best practice to initialize an array to zero or null while declaring if we don't assign any values to array.

## Types of C Arrays

Arrays are classified according to the number of subscripts present in the list. Based on this there are 2 types of C arrays. These are:

- One dimensional array

- Multi-dimensional array

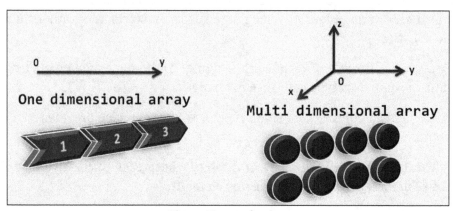

Figure: Types of array.

One dimensional array is used to represent and store data in a linear form. It has only one subscript in the variable name. It is also called as single dimensional or linear array. Many cases arrays having more than one subscript variable is used, which is known as multi-dimensional array. Such multi-dimensional array is also known as matrix. Let us now see how arrays are declared.

## Declaring Arrays

Arrays must be declared before it is used in C program like normal variables. The array declaration is nothing but defining the type of the array ( e.g. int, float, char etc.), name of the array, number of subscripts (i.e. whether one or multi-dimensional) and total number of memory locations to be allocated (i.e. maximum value of each subscript).

1. One Dimensional Array: The general syntax of one dimensional array is shown below.

**Syntax:** `<data type-of-array> <name-of-array> [<number of elements in array>];`

- Data type-of-array: It is the type of elements that an array stores. If array stores character elements then type of array is 'char'. If array stores integer elements then type of array is 'int'. Besides these native types, if type of elements in array is structure objects then type of array becomes the structure.

- Name-of-array: This is the name that is given to array. It can be any string but it is usually suggested that some standard should be followed while naming arrays. At least the name should be in context with what is being stored in the array.

- [Number of elements]: This value in subscripts [] indicates the number of elements the array stores.

For example: `int a[10];`

Table: One dimensional array.

| [0] | [1] | [2] | [3] | [4] | [5] | [6] | [7] | [8] | [9] |
|-----|-----|-----|-----|-----|-----|-----|-----|-----|-----|

Other similar declarations are:

`int rollno[100];`

`char name[20]`

`float distance[5];`

`double average[];`

2. Multi-dimensional Array: Although arrays with more than two dimensions are not commonly used, C language allow any size array to be declared. Please note that the exact limit is determined by the compiler. The general form of the multi-dimensional array is:

**Syntax:** `data_type array_name[array_size] ...... [array_size]`

Table: Two dimensional array.

|       | Col1    | Col2    | Col3    | Col4    | Col5    |
|-------|---------|---------|---------|---------|---------|
| Row1  | a[0][0] | a[0][1] | a[0][2] | a[0][3] | a[0][4] |
| Row2  | a[1][0] | a[1][1] | a[1][2] | a[1][3] | a[1][4] |

Some typical examples are:

`int a[3][3];`

`int table[2][3][4]`

`float graph[5][5][5];`

Let us consider the array 'table', which is a three dimensional array declared to contain 24 integers. The table may include data in 3-dimensions. Similarly, arrays with four, five, six dimensions and so on can be declared.

## Initializing an Array

Arrays can be initialized like ordinary variables either inside or outside the function. Arrays declared inside the function are local arrays and arrays declared outside the function are global arrays. Global arrays can be initialized when they are declared.

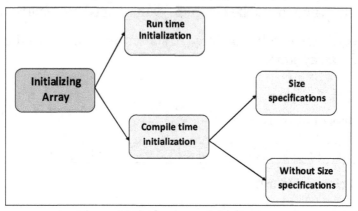

Figure: Methods of array initialization.

Let us understand these methods of initialization starting with compilation time initialization of an array.

Example: Array size specified

```
int a[5] = { 4,1,5,8,2};
```

In this example, the size of array is specified as 5 in the initialization/declaration statement. Compiler will assign these 5 values to an array 'a'.

Example: Array size unspecified

```
int a[] = { 4,1,5,8,2};
```

In this example, the size of an array is not specified in the initialization/ declaration statement. Here, compiler counts the number of elements written inside the pair of braces and determines the size of array. After counting the number of elements in an array, the size of any array is considered to be 5 during the execution of the program. Such method of initialization is known as compilation time initialization.

For example: `int a[] = {'1','2','3','4','5'};`

In the above example an array of five integers is declared. Note that since we are initializing at the time of declaration so there is no need to mention any value in the subscripts

[]. The size will automatically be calculated from the number of values. In this case, the size will be 5. An array can be initialized at run-time as shown in the following example. Here each element is initialized separately.

```
#include <stdio.h>

int main()

{

        int a[5];

        int i = 0;

        for(i=0;i<sizeof(a);i++)

        {

          a[i] = i; // Initializing each element separately

        }

        Return 0;

}
```

In this example, the array is initialized after compilation and during the run-time. Here each element is initialized separately. One can use printf statement to inform user that new array element is to be entered. This will help user to have a prompt before data entry.

## Initializing Array with a String

Method 1: Strings in C language are nothing but a series of characters followed by a null byte. So to store a string, we need an array of characters followed by a null byte. This makes the initialization of strings a bit different. Let us take a look:

Since strings are nothing but a series of characters so the array containing a string will be containing characters.

```
char arr[] = {'c','o','d','e','\0'};
```

In the above declaration/initialization, we have initialized array with a series of character followed by a '\0' (null) byte. The null byte is required as a terminating byte when string is read as a whole.

Method 2: Here we neither require to explicitly wrap single quotes around each character nor write a null character. The double quotes do the trick for us. For example:

```
char arr[] = "code";
```

```
int a[2][3]={{2,4,6}, {-5,8,9}};
```

OR

```
int c[][]={{2,4,6}, {-5,8,9}};
```

OR

```
int c[2][3]={ 2,4,6, -5,8,9};
```

After an array is declared it must be initialized. Otherwise, it will contain garbage value(any random value). An array can be initialized at either compile time or at run – time.

Two dimensional arrays can be initialized in the same manner like one dimensional array. While specifying the values during initialization it is written row wise. Brace pairs are used to separate the values of one row to next. For example:

```
int a[2][3] = {

{1, 2, 3},

{3, 4, 5}

};
```

Note that, special care be taken for defining the multi-dimensional array.

## Processing an Array

The first step in processing any array or an array element is to know the method to access individual array elements.

## Accessing Array Elements

In C programming, arrays can be accessed and treated like variables in C. For example:

```
scanf("%d",&a[3]);
```

This statement is used to obtain the 4 the element of array a[]. Here, the assumption is that the array is initialized from the oth element which is the first element of an array.

```
scanf("%d",&a[i]);
```

This statement is used to get the (i+1)[th] the element of array a[] from the keyboard. Here, the assumption is that the array is initialized from the o[th] element which is the first element of an array.

```
printf("%d",a[1]);
```

This statement is used to print the 2nd element of array a[]. Here, the assumption is that the array is initialized from the 0th element which is the first element of an array.

```
printf("%d",a[i]);
```

This statement is used to print (i+1)th lement of array a[]. Here, the assumption is that the array is initialized from the 0th element which is the first element of an array.

## Accessing Two-Dimensional Array Elements

Two dimensional array may be initialized and accessed just similar to one dimensional array. Following example demonstrates how to declare and initialize an array, printing an array with the help of two for loops.

```
#include <stdio.h>
int main ()
{
/* an array with 5 rows and 2 columns*/
int a[5][2] = { {0,0}, {1,1}, {2,2}, {3,3},{4,4}};
int i, j;
/* output each array element's value */
for ( i = 0; i < 5; i++ )
{
for ( j = 0; j < 2; j++ )
{
printf("a[%d][%d] = %d\n", i,j, a[i][j] );
}
}
return 0;
}
```

```
a[0][0]: 0
a[0][1]: 0
a[1][0]: 1
a[1][1]: 1
a[2][0]: 2
a[2][1]: 2
a[3][0]: 3
a[3][1]: 3
a[4][0]: 4
a[4][1]: 4
```

## Arithmetic Operations on Array

In this matrix format the arithmetic operation like addition can be performed where the matrix1 and matrix2 are being added together. In the matrix 1, there is 2 row and 2 column in which A11 defines the place of row1 and column1. Similarly for all other elements can also be designated and accessed like a11, a12, a21 and a22. This example shows how the values accessed and processed in the multi-dimensional arrays. Similar method may be adopted for subtraction of matrices.

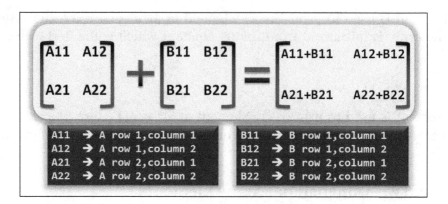

Let us consider a simple example to demonstrate arithmetic operations on two dimensional array:

```
Array1[2][2]={{1,2},{3,4}}
```

```
Array2[2][2]={{4,5},{2,4}}
```

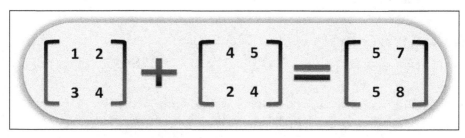

Here we see the example for addition of 2 by 2 matrices, here 1 is added with 4, 2 is added with 5 and so on.

Program for addition of two Matrices:

```
#include <stdio.h>

int main()

{

int a, b, i, j, M1[5][5], M2[5][5], sum[5][5];

printf("Enter the number of rows and columns of matrix:\n");

scanf("%d%d", &a, &b);

printf("Enter the elements of matrix M1:\n");

for (i = 0; i < a; i++)

for (j = 0; j < n; j++)
```

```
scanf("%d", &M1[i][j]);

printf("Enter the elements of matrix M2:\n");

for (i = 0; i < a; i++)

for (j = 0 ; j < b; j++)

scanf("%d", &M2[i][j]);

printf("Sum of entered matrices:\n");

for (i = 0; i < a; i++)

{

for (j = 0 ; j < n; j++)

{

sum[i][j] = M1[i][j] + M2[i][j];

printf("%d\t", sum[i][j]);

}

printf("\n");

}

return 0;

}
```

The result of the above program is shown here:

```
Enter the number of rows and columns of matrix:
2
2
Enter the elements of matrix M1:
1 2
3 4
Enter the elements of matrix M2:
2 4
6 1
Sum of entered matrices:
3 6
9 5
```

# Pointers

The Pointer in C is a variable that stores address of another variable. A pointer can also be used to refer to another pointer function. A pointer can be incremented/decremented, i.e., to point to the next/ previous memory location. The purpose of pointer is to save memory space and achieve faster execution time.

## How to Use Pointers in C

If we declare a variable v of type int, v will actually store a value.

```
int v = 0;
```

v is equal to zero now.

However, each variable, apart from value, also has its address (or, simply put, where it is located in the memory). The address can be retrieved by putting an ampersand (&) before the variable name.

```
&v
```

If you print the address of a variable on the screen, it will look like a totally random number (moreover, it can be different from run to run).

Pointer in C example:

```
#include <stdio.h>

int main() {
    int v = 0;
    printf("%d\n", &v);
    return 0;
}
```

The output of this program is -480613588.

## Pointer Variable

```
Int *y = &v;
```

| Variable | Pointer |
|---|---|
| A value stored in a named storage/memory address. | A variable that points to the storage/memory address of another variable. |

## Declaring a Pointer

Like variables, pointers in C programming have to be declared before they can be used in your program. Pointers can be named anything you want as long as they obey C's naming rules. A pointer declaration has the following form:

```
data_type * pointer_variable_name;
```

Here,

- `Data_type` is the pointer's base type of C's variable types and indicates the type of the variable that the pointer points to.

- The asterisk (*: the same asterisk used for multiplication) which is indirection operator, declares a pointer.

Let's see some valid pointer declarations in this C pointers:

```
int     *ptr_thing;             /* pointer to an integer */

int *ptr1,thing;/* ptr1 is a pointer to type integer and thing is an
integer variable */

double    *ptr2;    /* pointer to a double */

float     *ptr3;    /* pointer to a float */

char     *ch1 ;      /* pointer to a character */

float  *ptr, variable;/*ptr is a pointer to type float and variable is an
ordinary float variable */
```

## Initialize a Pointer

After declaring a pointer, we initialize it like standard variables with a variable address. If pointers in C programming are not uninitialized and used in the program, the results are unpredictable and potentially disastrous. To get the address of a variable, we use the ampersand (&)operator, placed before the name of a variable whose address we need. Pointer initialization is done with the following syntax.

Pointer Syntax:

```
pointer = &variable;
```

A simple program for pointer illustration is given below:

```
#include <stdio.h>

int main()
```

```
{

    int a=10;       //variable declaration

    int *p;         //pointer variable declaration

    p=&a;           //store address of variable a in pointer p

    printf("Address stored in a variable p is:%x\n",p);  //accessing the
address

     printf("Value stored in a variable p is:%d\n",*p);     //accessing
the value

    return 0;

}
```

Output:

```
Address stored in a variable p is:60ff08

Value stored in a variable p is:10
```

| Operator | Meaning |
|---|---|
| * | Serves 2 purpose<br>• Declaration of a pointer<br>• Returns the value of the referenced variable |
| & | Serves only 1 purpose<br>• Returns the address of a variable |

## Types of Pointers in C

Following are the different Types of Pointers in C:

## Null Pointer

We can create a null pointer by assigning null value during the pointer declaration. This method is useful when you do not have any address assigned to the pointer. A null pointer always contains value 0. Following program illustrates the use of a null pointer:

```
#include <stdio.h>

int main()

{

    int *p = NULL;     //null pointer
```

```
        printf("The value inside variable p is:\n%x",p);

        return 0;

}
```

Output:

```
The value inside variable p is:

0
```

## Void Pointer

In C programming, a void pointer is also called as a generic pointer. It does not have any standard data type. A void pointer is created by using the keyword void. It can be used to store an address of any variable. Following program illustrates the use of a void pointer:

```
#include <stdio.h>

int main()

{

void *p = NULL;    //void pointer

printf("The size of pointer is:%d\n",sizeof(p));

return 0;

}
```

## Wild Pointer

A pointer is said to be a wild pointer if it is not being initialized to anything. These types of C pointers are not efficient because they may point to some unknown memory location which may cause problems in our program and it may lead to crashing of the program. One should always be careful while working with wild pointers. Following program illustrates the use of wild pointer:

```
#include <stdio.h>

int main()

{

int *p;      //wild pointer

printf("\n%d",*p);
```

```
return 0;

}
```

Output:

```
timeout: the monitored command dumped core

sh: line 1: 95298 Segmentation fault      timeout 10s main
```

Other types of pointers in 'c' are as follows:

- Dangling pointer
- Complex pointer
- Near pointer
- Far pointer
- Huge pointer

## Direct and Indirect Access Pointers

In C, there are two equivalent ways to access and manipulate a variable content.

- Direct access: we use directly the variable name.
- Indirect access: we use a pointer to the variable

Let's understand this with the help of program below:

```c
#include <stdio.h>
/* Declare and initialize an int variable */
int var = 1;
/* Declare a pointer to int */
int *ptr;
int main( void )
{
/* Initialize ptr to point to var */
ptr = &var;
/* Access var directly and indirectly */
printf("\nDirect access, var = %d", var);
```

```
printf("\nIndirect access, var = %d", *ptr);
/* Display the address of var two ways */
printf("\n\nThe address of var = %d", &var);
printf("\nThe address of var = %d\n", ptr);
/*change the content of var through the pointer*/
*ptr=48;
printf("\nIndirect access, var = %d", *ptr);
return 0;}
```

After compiling the program without any errors, the result is:

```
Direct access, var = 1

Indirect access, var = 1

The address of var = 4202496

The address of var = 4202496

Indirect access, var = 48
```

## Pointer Arithmetic's in C

The pointer operations are summarized in the following figure.

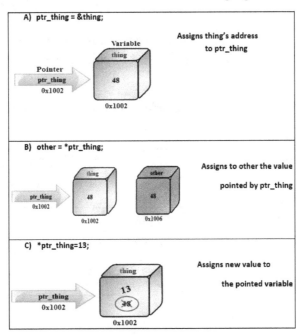

## Priority Operation (Precedence)

When working with C pointers, we must observe the following priority rules:

- The operators * and & have the same priority as the unary operators (the negation!, the incrementation++, decrement--).

- In the same expression, the unary operators *, &,!, ++, - are evaluated from right to left.

If a P pointer points to an X variable, then * P can be used wherever X can be written.

The following expressions are equivalent:

```
int X =10
```

```
int *P = &Y;
```

For the above code, below expressions are true.

| Expression | Equivalent Expression |
|------------|----------------------|
| Y=*P+1 | Y=X+1 |
| *P=*P+10 | X=X+10 |
| *P+=2 | X+=2 |
| ++*P | ++X |
| (*P)++ | X++ |

In the latter case, parentheses are needed: as the unary operators * and ++ are evaluated from right to left, without the parentheses the pointer P would be incremented, not the object on which P points.

Below table shows the arithmetic and basic operation that can be used when dealing with C pointers.

| Operation | Explanation |
|-----------|-------------|
| Assignment | int *P1,*P2 P1=P2; P1 and P2 point to the same integer variable |
| Incrementation and decrementation | Int *P1; P1++;P1-- ; |
| Adding an offset (Constant) | This allows the pointer to move N elements in a table. The pointer will be increased or decreased by N times the number of byte (s) of the type of the variable. P1+5; |

## C Pointers and Arrays with Examples

Traditionally, we access the array elements using its index, but this method can be eliminated by using pointers. Pointers make it easy to access each array element.

```c
#include <stdio.h>

int main()

{

    int a[5]={1,2,3,4,5};    //array initialization

    int *p;      //pointer declaration

            /*the ptr points to the first element of the array*/

    p=a; /*We can also type simply ptr==&a[0] */


    printf("Printing the array elements using pointer\n");

    for(int i=0;i<5;i++)     //loop for traversing array elements

    {

            printf("\n%x",*p);   //printing array elements

            p++;      //incrementing to the next element, you can also
write p=p+1

    }

    return 0;

}
```

Output:

1

2

3

4

5

Adding a particular number to a pointer will move the pointer location to the value obtained by an addition operation. Suppose p is a pointer that currently points to the memory location 0 if we perform following addition operation, p+1 then it will execute in this manner:

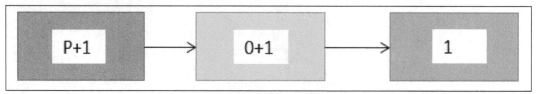

Figure: Pointer Addition/Increment

## C Pointers and Strings with Examples

A string is an array of char objects, ending with a null character '\ 0'. We can manipulate strings using pointers. This pointer in C example:

```c
#include <stdio.h>

#include <string.h>

int main()

{

char str[]="Hello Guru99!";

char *p;

p=str;

printf("First character is:%c\n",*p);

p =p+1;

printf("Next character is:%c\n",*p);

printf("Printing all the characters in a string\n");

p=str;   //reset the pointer

for(int i=0;i<strlen(str);i++)

{

printf("%c\n",*p);

p++;

}
```

```
return 0;

}
```

## Output:

```
First character is:H

Next character is:e

Printing all the characters in a string

H

e

l

l

o


G

u

r

u

9

9

!
```

Another way to deal strings is with an array of pointers like in the following program:

```
#include <stdio.h>

int main(){

char *materials[ ] = {  "iron",  "copper",  "gold"};

printf("Please remember these materials :\n");

int i ;

for (i = 0; i < 3; i++) {
```

```
printf("%s\n", materials[ i ]);}

return 0;}
```

Output:

```
Please remember these materials:

iron

copper

gold
```

## Advantages of Pointers in C

- Pointers are useful for accessing memory locations.

- Pointers provide an efficient way for accessing the elements of an array structure.

- Pointers are used for dynamic memory allocation as well as deallocation.

- Pointers are used to form complex data structures such as linked list, graph, tree, etc.

## Disadvantages of Pointers in C

- Pointers are a little complex to understand.

- Pointers can lead to various errors such as segmentation faults or can access a memory location which is not required at all.

- If an incorrect value is provided to a pointer, it may cause memory corruption.

- Pointers are also responsible for memory leakage.

- Pointers are comparatively slower than that of the variables.

- Programmers find it very difficult to work with the pointers; therefore it is programmer's responsibility to manipulate a pointer carefully.

# Structures

A group of one or more variables of different data types organized together under a single name is called Structure. A collection of heterogeneous (dissimilar) types of data grouped together under a single name is called a Structure.

A structure can be defined to be a group of logically related data items, which may be of different types, stored in contiguous memory locations, sharing a common name, but distinguished by its members.

Hence a structure can be viewed as a heterogeneous user-defined data type. It can be used to create variables, which can be manipulated in the same way as variables of built-in data types. It helps better organization and management of data in a program.

When a structure is defines the entire group s referenced through the structure name. The individual components present in the structure are called structure members and those can be accessed and processed separately.

## Structure Declaration

The declaration of a structure specifies the grouping of various data items into a single unit without assigning any resources to them. The syntax for declaring a structure in C is as follows:

struct Structure Name

```
{
        Data Type member-1;

        Data Type member-2;

        …. ….

        DataType member-n;
};
```

The structure declaration starts with the structure header, which consists of the keyword 'struct' followed by a tag. The tag serves as a structure name, which can be used for creating structure variables. The individual members of the structure are enclosed between the curly braces and they can be of the similar or dissimilar data types. The data type of each variable is specified in the individual member declarations.

Example:

Let us consider an employee database consisting of employee number, name, and salary. A structure declaration to hold this information is shown below:

```
struct employee

{
        int eno;
```

```
            char name [80];

            float sal;

};
```

The data items enclosed between curly braces in the above structure declaration are called structure elements or structure members.

Employee is the name of the structure and is called structure tag. Note that, some members of employee structure are integer type and some are character array type.

The individual members of a structure can be variables of built – in data types (int, char, float etc.), pointers, arrays, or even other structures. All member names within a particular structure must be different. However, member names may be the same as those of variables declared outside the structure. The individual members cannot be initialized inside the structure declaration.

Normally, structure declarations appear at the beginning of the program file, before any variables or functions are declared. They may also appear before the main ( ), along with macro definitions, such as #define. In such cases, the declaration is global and can be used by other functions as well.

## Structure Variables

Similar to other types of variables, the structure data type variables can be declared using structure definition.

```
struct

{

    int rollno;

    char name[20];

    float average;

     a, b;

}
```

In the above structure definition, a and b are said to be structure type variables. 'a' is a structure type variable containing rollno, name average as members, which are of different data types. Similarly 'b' is also a structure type variable with the same members of 'a '.

## Structure Initialization

The members of the structure can be initialized like other variables. This can be done at the time of declaration. For Example:

```
struct

{

  int day;

  int month;

  int year;

}

date = { 25,06,2012};

i.e

date. day = 25

date. month = 06

date. year = 2012

Example:

struct address

{

  char name [20];

  char desgn [10];

  char place [10];

} ;

i.e

struct address my-add = { 'Sree', 'AKM', 'RREDDY');

i.e

my-add . name = 'Sree'

my-add . desgn = AKM

my-add . place = RREDDY
```

The initial values for structure members must be enclosed with in a pair of curly braces. The values to be assigned to members must be placed in the same order as they are specified in structure definition, separated by commas. If some of the members of the structure are not initialized, then the c compiler automatically assigns a value 'zero' to them.

## Accessing of Structure Members

The structure can be individually identified using the period operator ( . ). After identification, we can access them by means of assigning some values to them as well as obtaining the stored values in structure members. The following program illustrates the accessing of the structure members.

Example: Write a C program, using structure definition to accept the time and display it.

```
/ * Program to accept time and display it */

# include <stdio.h>

main ( )

{

    struct

{

    int hour, min;

    float seconds;

  } time;

    printf ( "Enter time in Hours, min and Seconds\n");

    scanf ( " %d %d %f", &time . hour, & time . min, & time .     seconds);

    printf ( " The accepted time is %d %d %f " , time . hour, time . min, time

. seconds ");

}
```

## Nested Structures

The structure is going to certain number of elements /members of different data types. If the members of a structure are of structure data type, it can be termed as structure with structure or nested structure.

For Example:

```
struct
{
    int rollno;
    char name[20];
    float avgmarks;
    struct
{
    int day, mon, year;
} dob'
} student;
```

In the above declaration, student is a variable of structure type consisting of the members namely rollno, name, avgmarks and the structure variable dob. The dob structure is within another structure student and thus structure is nested. In this type of definitions, the elements of the require structure can be referenced by specifying appropriate qualifications to it, using the period operator ( . ).

For example, `student. dob. day` refers to the element day of the inner structure dob.

## Structures and Arrays

Array is group of identical stored in consecutive memory locations with a single / common variable name. This concept can be used in connection with the structure in the following ways.

- Array of structures.

- Structures containing arrays (or) arrays within a structure.

- Arrays of structures contain arrays.

## Array of Structures

Student details in a class can be stored using structure data type and the student details of entire class can be seen as an array of structure.

Example:

```
struct student

{

int rollno;

int year;

int tmarks;

}

struct student class[40];.
```

In the above class [40] is structure variable accommodating a structure type student up to 40. The above type of array of structure can be initialized as under:

```
struct student class [2] = { 001,2011,786},

{ 002, 2012, 710}

};

i.e  class[0] . rollno = 001

class[0] . year = 2011

class[0] . tmarks = 777 and

class[1] . rollno = 002

class[1] . year = 2012

class[1] . tmarks = 777 .
```

## Structures Containing Arrays

A structure data type can hold an array type variable as its member or members. We can declare the member of a structure as array data type similar to int, float or char. Example:

```
struct employee

{

    char ename [20];

    int eno;

};
```

In above, the structure variable employee contains character array type ename as its member. The initialization of this type can be done as usual.

```
struct employee = { ' Rajashekar', 7777};
```

## Arrays of Structures Contain Arrays

Arrays of structures can be defined and in that type of structure variables of array type can be used as members. For Example:

```
struct rk

{

    int empno;

    char ename[20];

    flat salary;

 } mark[50];
```

In the above, mark is an array of 50 elements and such element in the array is of structure type rk. The structure type rk, in turn contains ename as array type which is a member of the structure. Thus mark is an array of sutures and these structures in turn holds character names in array ename.

The initialization of the above type can be done as:

```
{

7777, ' Prasad' , 56800.00}

};

i.e mark[0] . empno = 7777;

 mark[0] . eame = 'Prasad';

 mark[0] . salary = 56800.00
```

## Program

Write a C program to accept the student name, rollno, average marks present in the class of student and to print the name of students whose average marks are greater than 40 by using structure concept with arrays.

```
# include <stdio.h>
```

```
main ( )
{
  int i, n,
  struct
  {
    char name [20];
    int rollno;
    flat avgmarks;
  }
class [40];
  printf (" Enter the no. of students in the class\n"0;
  scanf ( " %d", & n );
  for ( i = 0, i < n, i++)
{
    print ( " Enter students name, rollno, avgmarks\n");
    scanf ( " %s %d", &class[i].name, class[i].rollno, &class[i].avg-
marks)'
}
printf (" The name of the students whose average");
printf ( " marks is greater than 40 \n");
for ( i = 0, i < n, i++)
if ( class[i].avgmarks > 40)
pirintf (" %s", class[i].name);
}
```

## Advantages of Structure Type over Array Type Variables

- Using structures, we can group items of different types within a single entity, which is not possible with arrays, as array stores similar elements.

- The position of a particular structure type variable within a group is not needed in order to access it, whereas the position of an array member in the group is required, in order to refer to it.

- In order to store the data about a particular entity such as a 'Book', using an array type, we need three arrays, one for storing the 'name', another for storing the 'price' and a third one for storing the 'number of pages' etc., hence, the overhead is high. This overhead can be reduced by using structure type variable.

- Once a new structure has been defined, one or more variables can be declared to be of that type.

- A structure type variable can be used as a normal variable for accepting the user's input, for displaying the output etc.

- The assignment of one 'struct' variable to another, reduces the burden of the programmer in filling the variable's fields again and again.

- It is possible to initialize some or all fields of a structure variable at once, when it is declared.

- Structure type allows the efficient insertion and deletion of elements but arrays cause the inefficiency.

- For random array accessing, large hash tables are needed. Hence, large storage space and costs are required.

- When structure variable is created, all of the member variables are created automatically and are grouped under the given variable's name.

## Structure Contains Pointers

A pointer variable can also be used as a member in the structure. Example:

```
struct

{

    int *p1;

    int * p2;

} *rr;
```

In the above, *rr is a pointer variable of structure type which holds inside it another two pointer variables p1 and p2 as its members.

```
# include <stdio.h>
```

```
main ( )

{

 sturct

 int *p1, *p2;

} *rr;

int a, b ;

 a = 70;

 b = 100'

 rr — p1 = &a;

 rr — p2 = & b;

 printf( " The contents of pointer variables");

 printf( " Present in the structure as members are \n");

 printf ( '%d %d", *rr — p1, *rr — p2);

}
```

In the above program, two pointer variables p1 and p2 are declared as members of the structure and their contents / variables are printer after assignment in the program.

## Self-Referential Structures

Structures can have members which are of the type the same structure itself in which they are included, This is possible with pointers and the phenomenon is called as self-referential structures. A self-referential structure is a structure which includes a member as pointer to the present structure type.

The general format of self-referential structure is:

```
struct parent

{

    memeber1;

    memeber2;

    ————;

    ————;
```

```
    struct parent *name;

};
```

The structure of type parent is contains a member, which is pointing to another structure of the same type i.e. parent type and name refers to the name of the pointer variable. Here, name is a pointer which points to a structure type and is also an element of the same structure.

Example:

```
struct element

{

    char name{20};

  int num;

    struct element * value;

}
```

Element is of structure type variable. This structure contains three members:

- a 20 elements character array called name.

- An integer element called num.

- a pointer to another structure which is same type called value. Hence it is self-referential structure.

These structure are mainly used in applications where there is need to arrange data in ordered manner.

# C++ Programming Language

C++ is a programming language that is used to create high-performance applications and gives the programmers a high level of control over system resources and memory. C and C++ programming language is an interdisciplinary subject which makes it essential to understand its related fields.

C is a procedural language which is very powerful and mainly used in developing of system software like Operating system kernel, compilers, editors etc. and is also used for developing application software. Even though C is an excellent programming language, but it cannot model real world problems. In C language, once a program exceeds from 25,000 to 100,000 lines of code, it becomes so complex that it is difficult to take hold of as a whole. The solution for this type of problem has led to development of C++ language, in which the programmer has the ability to understand and manage larger, more complex programs. The C++ language has added object oriented features like classes, objects, inheritance, function overloading, operator overloading, virtual functions etc.

## Differences between C and C++

C++ is called superset of C as C++ extends C language. The major design criterion of C++ was to retain its compatibility with C. All valid C programs are C++ programs, hence a C++ compiler can compile and execute all C programs but the reverse is not true. The C++ language uses most of the features of C language such as decision-making statements, looping statements, structures. C++ supports the keywords of C language and C++ also contains some additional keywords which help in implementing object oriented paradigm. The major differences between C and C++ can be represented in the table as follows:

| C | C++ |
|---|---|
| C is a procedure oriented programming language where more emphasis is laid on procedures or algorithms rather than data. | C++ is object oriented programming where more emphasis is laid on data rather than on procedures or algorithms. |

| There is no strict type-checking in C. | Strict type-checking is done in C++, so many programs that run well in C compiler will result in errors and warnings under C++ compiler. |
|---|---|
| C supports only Early binding, in which all the functions related to the function call are resolved at compile time. All individual resolved function calls create an individual (.o) files which can be later linked together to create a final executable file. | C++ supports both Early binding and Late binding. Late binding is a process of resolving the functions related to the function call during run time. Here the functions are related to class much after the compilation time. It is also known as Dynamic binding. |
| Concept of default arguments is not available in C language. | Concept of default arguments is available in C++ language. |
| Functions cannot be overloaded. | Functions can be overloaded. |
| The memory management is done by the built-in functions, malloc, calloc, realloc, free. | The memory management is done by operators new and delete. |
| Declaration of the variables have to be done before the first executable statement within a block making the declaration of variables more rigid | Declaring of variables can be done at any point in the program wherever necessary, making declaration of variables more flexible compared to C language. |

## Features of C++

The C++ programming language is based on the C language. Although C++ is a descendant of the C language, the two languages are not always compatible. In C++, new data types can be developed that contain functional descriptions (member functions) as well as data representations. These new data types are called classes. The job of developing such classes is known as data abstraction. It is possible to work with a combination of classes from established class libraries, which helps to develop the classes according to the requirement, or derive new classes from existing classes by adding data descriptions and functions. The new classes can contain (inherit) properties from one or more classes. The classes describe the data types and functions available, but they can hide (encapsulate) the implementation details from the client programs. A series of functions can be defined with different argument types that all use the same function name. This is called function overloading. A function can have the same name and argument types in base and derived classes.

A class member function can be declared in a base class which allows to override its implementation in a derived class. With the help of virtual functions, class-dependent behavior may be determined at run time. This ability to select functions at run time, depending on data types, is called polymorphism. The meaning of the basic language operators can be redefined so that they can perform operations on user-defined classes (new data types), in addition to operations on system-defined data types, such as int, char, and float. Adding properties to operators for new data types is called operator overloading.

The C++ language provides templates and several keywords which are not found in the C language. It also include features such as try-catch-throw exception handling, stricter type checking and more versatile access to data and functions compared to the C language.

## Keywords in C++

Keywords are reserved words whose meaning is already been defined for a particular language. The keywords cannot be used as variable names. The keywords that are available in C++ language can be represented in the table as follows:

| asm | explicit | protected | typeid |
|---|---|---|---|
| auto | export | public | typename |
| break | extern | register | union |
| case | false | reinterpret_cast | unsigned |
| catch | float | return | using |
| char | for | short | virtual |
| class | friend | signed | void |
| const | goto | sizeof | volatile |
| const_cast | if | static | wchar_t |
| continue | inline | static_cast | while |
| default | int | struct | |
| delete | long | switch | |
| do | main | template | |
| dynamic_cast | mutable | this | |
| else | namespace | throw | |
| enum | new | true | |
| | operator | try | |
| | private | typedef | |

## Header File Specification

When a library function is included in the program, it is must to include its header. It is done using the #include statement.

Example: In C language, to include the header for the I/O functions, it is must to include stdio.h with a statement as follows:

```
#include <stdio.h>
```

In the above line of code, `stdio.h` is the name of the file used by the I/O functions, and the preceding statement causes that file to be included in the program.

When C++ was first invented and for several years after that, C++ used the same style of headers as that of C language, that is, it used header files. The Standard C++ supports C-style headers for header files like "`iostream.h`", "`fstream.h`" to maintain backward compatibility. On the other hand, standard C++ created a new kind of header that is used by the Standard C++ library. Example:

```
#include <iostream.h>
```

The above line of code causes the file `iostream.h` to be included in the program.

The new-style headers do not specify filenames. Instead, they simply specify standard identifiers that may be mapped to files by the compiler, even though they need not be. The new-style C++ headers are an abstraction that simply guarantees that the suitable prototypes and definitions required by the C++ library have been declared. Since the new-style headers are not filenames, they do not have an .h extension. They consist of only of the header name contained between angle brackets.

Some of the new versions of header files are as follows:

| Old Version | New Version |
| --- | --- |
| <assert.h.> | <cassert> |
| <ctype.h> | <cctype> |
| <float.h> | <cfloat> |
| <limits.h> | <climits> |
| <math.h> | <cmath> |
| <stdio.h> | <cstdio> |
| <stdlib.h> | <cstdlib> |
| <string,h> | <cstring> |
| <time.h> | <ctime> |

In general, an old-style header file will use the same name as its corresponding new-style header with an .h appended.

## C++ Output/Input

The main aim of any programming language is to help the user to do certain operations, which include, user giving some input to the system, using which, processor does some operations and gives back the user the result. Since user cannot speak the hardware language, the high level language like C++ is used as a means of communication by the user which will be later converted into hardware language during compilation process to communicate to the hardware.

## Console Input

The binary operator ">>" is also known as extraction operator which is used to get the data from the object on its left, i.e., the standard input stream , and tries to store in the memory location associated with it using variables towards its right. This operator is bitwise right-shift operator but it has been overloaded to make it work as extraction operator.

Example: `cin>>x;`

The above statement waits for the user to enter a value through the keyboard.

## Console Output

The cout is used to write the characters on to the standard output stream. The operator "<<" , which is a binary operator sends the contents of the variable on its right to the object on its left. The operator "<<" is also called as insertion operator. This operator is actually bitwise left-shift  operator but it has been overloaded to make it work as insertion operator. The advantage of insertion operator is that it does not require any format specifiers like %d, %c. %f etc .as in C language to represent the data of different data types.

Example: `cout<<"x = "<<x<<endl;`

The above statement tries to write the value of x on the screen or monitor.

## Variables

A variable is a memory location reserved for use by the program and is referenced by a specific name. The variables contain values that can be modified during the program execution. The values may be data of different types such as int, float, double etc. Before using the variable, it should be declared by stating the data type of value that the variable contains. In C, all the variables has to be defined at the beginning of scope i.e., above all executable statements, whereas in C++, declaration can be done anywhere in the scope, i.e., variable can be specified where it has to be used. While naming a variable, it must be remembered that, the variable name should not be a keyword and whitespaces are not allowed in variable name. The variable name may contain a letter, digit and an underscore (_) character. The syntax to declare a variable is as follows:

```
<Datatype> <variable_name>;
```

or

The syntax to declare and define a variable is as follows:

```
<Datatype> <variable_name>=<value>;
```

Program to print the value of the variables:

```
#include<iostream>

int main()

{
        int i;

        i = 10;

        cout<<"i = "<<i <<endl;

        int j;

        j=20;

        cout<<"j = "<<j <<endl;

        return 0;
}
```

When the above code is compiled and executed, it produces the following result:

i = 10

j = 20

## Initialization of Variable

When declaring a regular local variable, its value is by default undetermined. But if the task is that a variable should store a concrete value at the same moment that it is declared. In order to do that, it is possible to initialize the variable. There are two ways to initialize a variable in C++, they are as follows:

## C-Like Initialization

It is done by appending an equal sign followed by the value to which the variable will be initialized:

```
type identifier = initial_value ;

Example: int a = 0;
```

## Constructor Initialization

It is done by enclosing the initial value between parentheses (()):

Syntax: `type identifier (initial_value);`

Example: `int a (0);` Both ways of initializing variables are valid and equivalent in C++. Program to implement the usage of initialization of variables:

```cpp
#include <iostream>

int main ()

{
     int a=5;

      int b(2);

      int result;

      a = a + 3;

      result = a - b;

      cout << result;

       return 0;

}
```

When the above code is compiled and executed, it produces the following result:

6

## Reference Variables

A reference variable is an implicit pointer. A reference variable is a reference or alias for a previously defined variable. The memory location of the already existing variable is shared by the reference variable. The reference variable should not be initialized to address of an object. The syntax for declaring a reference variable is as follows:

`<data_type> & <reference_variable> = <existing_variable>`

Where,

`<data_type>` → is the type of data to which the reference variable is implicitly pointing.

`&` → is known as reference operator.

`<reference_variable>` → is the new variable which is pointing to the already exisiting variable and acts as reference.

`=` → is known as assignment operator.

`<existing_variable>` → is the previously defined variable which originally holds the data.

## Features of Reference Variable in C++

- A reference variable must be initialized at the time of declaration itself.

- Once a reference is made for a variable, it cannot be made to refer to any other variable.

- A variable and its reference are bonded strongly, such that a change in one necessarily results in a change in other.

- Like int, float and double, the reference variable can also be made to reference pointer.

- The major advantage of reference variables is in passing them as arguments to functions, this have a greater advantage of over passing the address of variables to functions as pointers.

- A function can also return by reference.

- A reference to an array is allowed in C++.

Program to implement the usage of reference variable:

```
#include <iostream>

int main ()

{

int i;

double d;

int& r = i;

double& s = d;

i = 5;

cout << "Value of i : " << i << endl;

cout << "Value of i reference : " << r <<endl;
```

```
d = 11.7;

cout << "Value of d : "<< d << endl;

cout << "Value of d reference : " << s <<endl;

return 0;

}
```

When the above code is compiled and executed, it produces the following result:

```
Value of i : 5

Value of i reference: 5

Value of d : 11.7

Value of d reference : 11.7
```

## Namespaces

When a new-style header is included in the program, the contents of that header are contained in the std namespace. A namespace is simply a declarative region. The purpose of a namespace is to restrict the names of identifiers to avoid name conflicts. The elements declared in one namespace are separate from elements declared in another. Initially, the names of the C++ library functions, etc., were simply put into the global namespace, as they are in C. But with the advent of the new-style headers, the contents of these headers were placed in the std namespace. It is must to include using directive for using the identifiers defined in the namespace scope. Its syntax is as follows:

```
using namespace <namespace_name>;
```

Example: `using namespace std;`

The above statement brings the std namespace into visibility, i.e., it puts std into the global namespace. After this statement has been compiled, there is no difference between working with an old-style header and a new-style one. When a C++ program includes a C header, such as stdio.h, its contents are put into the global namespace. This allows a C++ compiler to compile C subset programs.

Program to implement the usage of namespace:

```
#include<iostream>

using namespace std;

int main()

{
```

```
int i,j,sum;

cout<<"enter the values for i and j"<<endl;

cin>>i>>j;

sum=i+j;

cout<<" i is "<<i<<" j is "<<j<<" sum is "<<sum<<endl;

return 0;
}
```

When the above code is compiled and executed, it produces the following result: enter the values for i and j.

10

20

i is 10 j is 20 sum is 30.

## Function Prototyping

Function prototyping is a declaration statement in the calling program which describes the function's interface to the compiler by giving details such as number of arguments passed, data type of arguments, data type of value that function returns. The syntax of function prototyping is as follows:

```
<return_type> <function_name> <argument_list>
```

Where,

`<return_type>` is the type of the data the function is expected to return to the calling function.

`<function_name>` is the name of the function and should be a valid identifier.

`<argument_list>` contains the type of data (int, float, double etc) the function call passes as arguments to the function definition.

With function prototyping, during a function call, the compiler uses the function prototype to ensure that proper arguments are passed and the return value is handled, and if not, compiler identifies its during compilation time itself and displays the error message, because C++ is strict in type checking.

An example of function prototyping is as follows: `float add(int x, float y);`

The above statement tells compiler that add is a function which passes two parameters, first one being int and second one being float, and the function add() returns the value of floating point type to the calling function. The above example can also be written as follows:

```
float add(int , float);
```

The argument name is not required, it just acts as a placeholder for the values. The compiler mainly looks for the type of arguments and it does not matter whether the argument name is specified or not. Program to implement the usage of function prototyping:

```cpp
#include<iostream.h>

float add (int , float) ; // function prototype

int main ()

{

int x =2 ;

float y = 3.6, z ;

z = add(x,y) ;

cout<<"x = "<<x << " y = "<<y <<" z= "<<z <<endl;

return 0;

}

float add(int a, float b)

{

return (a+b);

}
```

When the above code is compiled and executed, it produces the following result:

x = 2 y = 3.6 z= 5.6

## Function Overloading

In C++ programming, it is allowed to create two or more functions with the same name but their parameter declarations should be different. Hence, the functions that share the same name are said to be overloaded and the process is called as function overloading. It is also known as function polymorphism in OOP. It is possible for the user to create a set of functions with same names but number and types of parameter list should be different in each function with the help of function overloading. The correct function to be invoked is determined by checking the number and type of the arguments but not on the return type of the function. Hence function prototype is much necessary and it tries to match a function call to the correct function definition. The compiler tries to implement BEST MATCHING strategy while performing function overloading on functions, and the strategy is as follows:

- Looks for the exact match of a function prototype with that of a function call statement.

- In case an exact match is unavailable, it tries to look for nearest exact match, i.e., the compiler will perform integral data promotions and then match the call statement with the function prototype.

- If neither of the case works, then it tries to give an error message.

## Rules for Function Overloading

- Each overloaded function must differ either by number of its formal parameters, their data types or sequence of the parameters.

- The default arguments of the overloaded functions are not considered as a part of the parameter list by C++ Compiler.

- The return type of overloaded functions may or may not be same.

Program to implement the usage of function overloading:

```cpp
#include<iostream>

using namespace std;

int add(int, int);

float add(int, float);

int main()

{

int x1 = 2, x2 = 3;

float f1 = 2.2;

int d,e;

e = add(x1,x2);

float f3 = add(x2,f1);

cout <<"x1 = "<<x1<<"x2 = "<<x2<<"e = "<<e<<endl;
```

```
cout <<"x2 = "<<x2<<"f1 = "<<f1<<"f3 = "<<f3<<endl;

return 0;

}

int add(int i1, int i2)

{

return (i1+i2);

}

float add(int i, float f)

{

return (i+f);

}
```

When the above code is compiled and executed, it produces the following result:

```
X1 = 2 x2=3          e = 5 x2 = 3              f1=2.2                    f3=5.2
```

Program to find absolute value of a number using function overloading:

```
#include <iostream>

using namespace std;

int abs(int i);

double abs(double d);

long abs(long l);

int main()

{

cout << abs(-10) << "\n";

cout << abs(-11.0) << "\n";

cout << abs(-9L) << "\n";

return 0;

}
```

```
int abs(int i)

{

cout << "Using integer abs()\n";

return i<0 ? -i : i;

}

double abs(double d)

{

cout << "Using double abs()\n";

return d<0.0 ? -d : d;

}

long abs(long l)

{

cout << "Using long abs()\n";

return l<0 ? -l : l;

}
```

When the above code is compiled and executed, it produces the following result:

```
Using integer abs()

10

Using double abs()

11

Using long abs()

9
```

## Default Arguments

It is a concept of C++ in which a function assigns a default values for some or all of formal arguments which does not have a matching argument in the function call, these default values are called as "default arguments". This allows us to call a function without assigning all its arguments. If no value is passed for any of the formal arguments when the function is called, the default value specified in the function prototype is passed to the corresponding formal argument and if all arguments are passed when the function is called then the default value is ignored.

## Features of Default Arguments

- Default arguments can be assigned to more than one argument.

- Default arguments can be used to add new parameters to the existing functions.

- Defaults arguments can be used to combine similar functions into one.

Program to implement the usage of default arguments:

```cpp
#include<iostream.h>

int vol(int=1,int=2,int=3);

int main()

{

int length;

int width;

int height;

int volume;

length=5;

width=4;

height=12;

volume=vol();

cout<<"\n Volume with no argument passed = "<<volume<<endl;

volume=vol(length);

cout<<"\n Volume with one argument passed = "<<volume<<endl;

volume=vol(length,width);

cout<<"\n Volume with two argument passed = "<<volume<<endl;

volume=vol(length,width,height);

cout<<"\n Volume with all argument passed = "<<volume<<endl;
```

```
return 0;

}

int vol(int l,int h,int w)

{

return l*h*w;

}
```

When the above code is compiled and executed, it produces the following result:

- Volume with no argument passed = 6

- Volume with one argument passed = 30

- Volume with two argument passed = 60

- Volume with all argument passed = 240

## Inline Functions

The Objective of using functions in programs is to save a memory space, that becomes appreciable when function is likely to be called many times. If function is called every time, it takes a lot of extra time in executing a series of instructions for tasks like jumping to a function, saving registers, pushing arguments into the stack, and returning to the calling function. When function is small, a substantial percentage of execution time may be spent in such overheads. One solution given by C is the use macro preprocessor feature, but the drawback is that they are not really functions, so error checking does not occur during compilation. But C++ overcomes this problem by introducing a new feature called inline function. It eliminates the cost of calls to small functions. An inline function is a function that is expanded in line when it is invoked. The compiler replaces the function call with the corresponding function code. The syntax to define inline function is as follows:

```
inline function-header

{

function-body

}
```

Example:

```
inline double cube(double a)

{
```

```
return (a*a*a);

}
```

The above inline function can be invoked by statements like

c=cube(3.0);

d=cube(2.5+1.5);

After execution the value of c and d will be 27 and 64.

It is easy to make the function inline, all that is required is to add prefix inline to the function definition. All inline functions must be defined before they are called. The functions are made inline when they are small enough to be defined in one or two lines. Some of situations where inline expansions may not work are:

- For functions returning values, if loop, a switch or a goto exists.
- For functions not returning values, if a return statement exists.
- If functions contain static variables.
- If inline functions are recursive.

Program to illustrate the use of inline functions:

```
#include<iostream>

inline float cube(float value)

{

return value*value*value;

}

int main()

{

float number=1.2;

cout<<"\n The cube of the number "<<number<<" = "<<cube(number)<<endl;

return 0;

}
```

When the above code is compiled and executed, it produces the following result:

The cube of the number 1.2 = 1.728

# Algorithms in C++

The algorithm library provides several functions that can be used for a variety of purposes, for instance searching, sorting, counting, manipulating and so on. These functions operate on ranges of elements and the range is defined as [first, last].

Here we introduce the reader to four main algorithmic paradigms: complete search, greedy algorithms, divide and conquer, and dynamic programming. Many algorithmic problems can be mapped into one of these four categories and the mastery of each one will make you a better programmer.

## Complete Search

Complete search (aka brute force or recursive backtracking) is a method for solving a problem by traversing the entire search space in search of a solution. During the search we can prune parts of the search space that we are sure do not lead to the required solution. In programming contests, complete search will likely lead to Time Limit Exceeded (TLE), however, it's a good strategy for small input problems.

### Complete Search Example: 8 Queens Problem

Our goal is to place 8 queens on a chess board such that no two queens attack each other. In the most naive solution, we would need to enumerate 64 choose 8 ~ 4B possibilities. A better naive solution is to realize that we can put each queen in a separate column, which leads to $8^8$~17M possibilities. We can do better by placing each queen in a separate column and a separate row that results in 8!~40K valid row permutations. In the implementation below, we assume that each queen occupies a different column, and we compute a valid row number for each of the 8 queens.

```cpp
#include <cstdlib>

#include <cstdio>

#include <cstring>
using namespace std; //row[8]: row # for each queen
//TC: traceback counter
//(a, b): 1st queen placement at (r=a, c=b)
int row[8], TC, a, b, line_counter; bool place(int r, int c)
{
    // check previously placed queens
    for (int prev = 0; prev < c; prev++)
    {
        // check if same row or same diagonal
        if (row[prev] == r || (abs(row[prev] - r) == abs(prev - c)))
```

```
                return false;
        }
        return true;
}void backtrack(int c)
{
        // candidate solution; (a, b) has 1 initial queen
        if (c == 8 && row[b] == a)
        {
                printf("%2d %d", ++line_counter, row[0] + 1);
                for (int j=1; j < 8; j++) {printf(" %d", row[j] + 1);}
                printf("\n");
        }    //try all possible rows
        for (int r = 0; r < 8; r++)
        {
                if (place(r, c))
                {
                        row[c] = r; // place a queen at this col and row
                        backtrack(c + 1); //increment col and recurse
                }
        }
}int main()
{
        scanf("%d", &TC);
        while (TC--)
        {
                scanf("%d %d", &a, &b); a--; b--; //0-based indexing
                memset(row, 0, sizeof(row)); line_counter = 0;
                printf("SOLN COLUMN\n");
                printf(" # 1 2 3 4 5 6 7 8\n\n");
                backtrack(0); //generate all possible 8! candidate solutions
                if (TC) printf("\n");
        }
        return 0;
}
```

For TC=8 and an initial queen position at (a,b) = (1,1) the above code results in the following output:

```
SOLN    COLUMN
   #     1 2 3 4 5 6 7 8
   1     1 5 8 6 3 7 2 4
   2     1 6 8 3 7 4 2 5
   3     1 7 4 6 8 2 5 3
   4     1 7 5 8 2 4 6 3
```

which indicates that there are four possible placements given the initial queen position at (r=1,c=1). Notice that the use of recursion allows to more easily prune the search space in comparison to an iterative solution.

## Greedy Algorithms

A greedy algorithm takes a locally optimum choice at each step with the hope of eventually reaching a globally optimal solution. Greedy algorithms often rely on a greedy heuristic and one can often find examples in which greedy algorithms fail to achieve the global optimum.

## Greedy Example: Fractional Knapsack

A greedy knapsack problem consists of selecting what items to place in a knapsack of limited capacity W so as to maximize the total value of knapsack items, where each item has an associated weight and value. We can define a greedy heuristic to be a ratio of item value to item weight, i.e. we would like to greedily choose items that are simultaneously high value and low weight and sort the items based on this criteria. In the fractional knapsack problem, we are allowed to take fractions of an item (as opposed to 0–1 Knapsack).

```cpp
#include <iostream>
#include <algorithm>
using namespace std; struct Item{
    int value, weight;
    Item(int value, int weight) : value(value), weight(weight) {}
}; bool cmp(struct Item a, struct Item b){
    double r1 = (double) a.value / a.weight;
    double r2 = (double) b.value / b.weight;
    return r1 > r2;
} double fractional_knapsack(int W, struct Item arr[], int n)
{
    sort(arr, arr + n, cmp);       int cur_weight = 0; double tot_value
= 0.0;
    for (int i=0; i < n; ++i)
    {
        if (cur_weight + arr[i].weight <= W)
        {
            cur_weight += arr[i].weight;
            tot_value += arr[i].value;
        }
        else
        {   //add a fraction of the next item
            int rem_weight = W - cur_weight;
```

```
                tot_value += arr[i].value *
                            ((double) rem_weight / arr[i].weight);
            break;
        }
    }
    return tot_value;
}
int main()
{
    int W = 50; // total knapsack weight
    Item arr[] = {{60, 10}, {100, 20}, {120, 30}}; //{value, weight}
    int n = sizeof(arr) / sizeof(arr[0]);
    cout << "greedy fractional knapsack" << endl;
    cout << "maximum value: " << fractional_knapsack(W, arr, n);
    cout << endl;
    return 0;
}
```

Since sorting is the most expensive operation, the algorithm runs in O(n log n) time. Given (value, weight) pairs of three items: {(60, 10), (100, 20), (120, 30)}, and the total capacity W=50, the code above produces the following output:

```
greedy fractional knapsack
maximum value: 240
```

We can see that the input items are sorted in decreasing ratio of value/cost, after greedily selecting items 1 and 2, we take a 2/3 fraction of item 3 for a total value of 60+100+(2/3)120 = 240.

## Divide and Conquer

Divide and Conquer (D&C) is a technique that divides a problem into smaller, independent sub-problems and then combines solutions to each of the sub-problems. Examples of divide and conquer technique include sorting algorithms such as quick sort, merge sort and heap sort as well as binary search.

### D&C Example: Binary Search

The classic use of binary search is in searching for a value in a sorted array. First, we check the middle of the array to see if if contains what we are looking for. If it does or there are no more items to consider, we stop. Otherwise, we decide whether the answer is to the left or the right of the middle element and continue searching. As the size of the search space is halved after each check, the complexity of the algorithm is O(log n).

```cpp
#include <algorithm>
#include <vector>
#include <iostream>
using namespace std;int bsearch(const vector<int> &arr, int l, int r,
int q)
{
    while (l <= r)
    {
        int mid = l + (r-l)/2;
        if (arr[mid] == q) return mid;

        if (q < arr[mid]) { r = mid - 1; }
        else              { l = mid + 1; }
    }
    return -1; //not found
}int main()
{
    int query = 10;
    int arr[] = {2, 4, 6, 8, 10, 12};
    int N = sizeof(arr)/sizeof(arr[0]);
    vector<int> v(arr, arr + N);

    //sort input array
    sort(v.begin(), v.end());       int idx;
    idx = bsearch(v, 0, v.size(), query);
    if (idx != -1)
        cout << "custom binary_search: found at index " << idx;
    else
        cout << "custom binary_search: not found";     return 0;
}
```

The code above produces the following output:

```
custom binary_search: found at index 4
```

If the query element is not found but we would like to find the first entry not smaller than the query or the first entry greater than the query, we can use STL lower_bound and upper_bound.

## Dynamic Programming

Dynamic Programming (DP) is a technique that divides a problem into smaller over-lapping sub-problems, computes a solution for each sub-problem and stores it in a DP table. The final solution is read off the DP table. Key skills in mastering dynamic programming is the ability to determine the problem states (entries of the DP table) and the relationships or transitions between the states. Then, having defined base cases and recursive relationships, one can populate the DP table in a top-down or bottom-up fashion.

In the top-down DP, the table is populated recursively, as needed, starting from the top and going down to smaller sub-problems. In the bottom-up DP, the table is populated iteratively starting from the smallest sub-problems and using their solutions to build-on and arrive at solutions to bigger sub-problems. In both cases, if a sub-problem was already encountered, its solution is simply looked up in the table (as opposed to re-computing the solution from scratch). This dramatically reduces computational cost.

## DP Example: Binomial Coefficients

We use binomial coefficients example to illustrate the use of top-down and bottom-up DP. The code below is based on the recursion for binomial coefficients with overlapping sub-problems. Let C(n,k) denote n choose k, then, we have:

```
Base case: C(n,0) = C(n,n) = 1
```

```
Recursion: C(n,k) = C(n-1, k-1) + C(n-1, k)
```

Notice that we have multiple over-lapping sub-problems. E.g. For C(n=5, k=2) the recursion tree is as follows:

```
                                    C(5, 2)
                        /                              \
           C(4, 1)                                        C(4, 2)
          /       \                                      /       \
   C(3, 0)    C(3, 1)                         C(3, 1)               C(3, 2)
             /      \                        /      \              /      \
        C(2, 0)  C(2, 1)              C(2, 0) C(2, 1)      C(2, 1)   C(2, 2)
                /      \                     /    \        /    \
           C(1, 0)  C(1, 1)            C(1, 0)  C(1, 1) C(1, 0)  C(1, 1)
```

We can implement top-down and bottom-up DP as follows:

```cpp
#include <iostream>
#include <cstring>
using namespace std; #define V 8
int memo[V][V]; //DP table int min(int a, int b) {return (a < b) ? a
: b;} void print_table(int memo[V][V])
{
    for (int i = 0; i < V; ++i)
```

```
    {
        for (int j = 0; j < V; ++j)
        {
            printf(" %2d", memo[i][j]);
        }
        printf("\n");
    }
} int binomial_coeffs1(int n, int k)
{
    // top-down DP
    if (k == 0 || k == n) return 1;
    if (memo[n][k] != -1) return memo[n][k];
    return memo[n][k] = binomial_coeffs1(n-1, k-1) +
                        binomial_coeffs1(n-1, k);
}int binomial_coeffs2(int n, int k)
{
    // bottom-up DP
    for (int i = 0; i <= n; ++i)
    {
        for (int j = 0; j <= min(i, k); ++j)
        {
            if (j == 0 || j == i)
            {
                memo[i][j] = 1;
            }
            else
            {
                memo[i][j] = memo[i-1][j-1] + memo[i-1][j];
            }
        }
    }
    return memo[n][k];
}
int main()
{
    int n = 5, k = 2;
    printf("Top-down DP:\n");
    memset(memo, -1, sizeof(memo));
    int nCk1 = binomial_coeffs1(n, k);
    print_table(memo);
    printf("C(n=%d, k=%d): %d\n", n, k, nCk1);

    printf("Bottom-up DP:\n");
```

```
    memset(memo, -1, sizeof(memo));
    int nCk2 = binomial_coeffs2(n, k);
    print_table(memo);
    printf("C(n=%d, k=%d): %d\n", n, k, nCk2);

    return 0;
}
```

For C(n=5, k=2), the code above produces the following output:

```
Top-down DP:
 -1 -1 -1 -1 -1 -1 -1 -1
 -1 -1 -1 -1 -1 -1 -1 -1
 -1  2 -1 -1 -1 -1 -1 -1
 -1  3  3 -1 -1 -1 -1 -1
 -1  4  6 -1 -1 -1 -1 -1
 -1 -1 10 -1 -1 -1 -1 -1
 -1 -1 -1 -1 -1 -1 -1 -1
 -1 -1 -1 -1 -1 -1 -1 -1
C(n=5, k=2): 10Bottom-up DP:
  1 -1 -1 -1 -1 -1 -1 -1
  1  1 -1 -1 -1 -1 -1 -1
  1  2  1 -1 -1 -1 -1 -1
  1  3  3 -1 -1 -1 -1 -1
  1  4  6 -1 -1 -1 -1 -1
  1  5 10 -1 -1 -1 -1 -1
 -1 -1 -1 -1 -1 -1 -1 -1
 -1 -1 -1 -1 -1 -1 -1 -1
C(n=5, k=2): 10
```

The time complexity is $O(n * k)$ and the space complexity is $O(n * k)$. In the case of top-down DP, solutions to sub-problems are stored (memoized) as needed, whereas in the bottom-up DP, the entire table is computed starting from the base case. Note: a small DP table size (V=8) was chosen for printing purposes, a much larger table size is recommended.

## C++ Program Structure

A C++ program can be developed from a basic structure. The general structure of C++ program with classes is also called overview of a C++ program, it is as follows:

- Documentation Section

- Preprocessor Directives or Compiler Directives Section

  ○ Link Section

  ○ Definition Section

- Global Declaration Section

- Class declaration or definition

- Main C++ program function called main ( )

- Beginning of the program: Left brace {

  ○ Object declaration part

  ○ Accessing member functions (using dot operator)

- End of the main program: Right brace }

## Documentation Section

The Documentation section consists of Heading and Comments. The heading can be specified using comments. Comment statement is the non-executable statement and it can be defined either by using single-line comment or multiple-line comment. Example:

```
//Add Two Numbers (Heading of the program)

//Program to find the square root of a number

/* Write a C++ program

to find the sum and

average of five numbers. */
```

## Preprocessor Directives

These are compiler preprocessor statements. These are also optional statements, but becomes compulsory if the compiler has INCLUDE and LIB subdirectories in the specified drive TCPLUS or having any name. The Pre-compiler statements are of two types, they are:

## Link Section

It is possible to link the compiler function like cout<>, sqrt ( ), fmod ( ), sleep ( ), clrscr ( ), exit(), strcat() etc. with the INCLUDE subdirectory having header files like iostream.h, conio.h, math.h, dos.h, string.h, `ctype.h,` `process.h` etc. These are very useful during the compilation and the linkage phase.

Syntax:

```
#include <header file>
```

```
or
```

```
#include "header file"
```

Example:

```
#include <iostream.h>
```

```
#include <conio.h>
```

## Definition Section

This section is used to define a variable with its value. The define statement is used to perform the task.

Syntax: #define variable name value

Example:

#define PI 3.142

#define A 100

#define NAME "tom"

## Global Declaration Section

This section can be used to declare some variables before starting of the main program or outside the main program. These variables are globally declared and used by the main function or sub function. These variables are called global variables. The global variables are automatically initialized with zero, hence there is no chance of garbage value.

Syntax:

data type vl,v2,v3.......... vn;

In the above syntax, data types are int, float, char, double etc. vl,v2,v3, .... vn is the list of global variables(v).

## Class Declaration

A class is way to bind the data and its associated functions together. A class is an organization of data and functions which operate on them. The combination of data members and member functions constitute a data object or simply an object. It allows data and functions to be hidden, if necessary from external use. When defining a class, a new abstract data type can be created that can be treated like any other built-in data type.

The general syntax or general form of the class declaration is as follows:

```
class <name of class>

{

private:

data members;

member functions ();

public:

data members;

member functions ();

protected:

data members;

member functions ();

};

int main()

{

<name of class> obj1;

obj1.member function ();

obj1.member function();

return 0;

}
```

## Class Name or Name of Class

It is mainly the name given to a particular class. It serves as a name specifier for the class, using which objects can be created. The class is specified by keyword "class".

Syntax: `class <class_name>`

Example:

```
class circle
```

## Data Members

These are the data-type properties that describe the characteristics of a class. It is possible that any number of data members of any type can be declared in a class.

Example:

```
float radius;
```

```
float area;
```

## Member Functions

The functions that are defined in the class are called as member functions. Any number of member functions of any type can be declared in a class. The member functions are accessed using object and dot operator.

Example:

```
void read();
```

```
void display();
```

## Access Specifiers

Access Specifiers are used to identify access rights for the data members and member functions of the class. Depending upon the access level of a class member, the access to it is allowed or it is denied. The three different types of access specifiers are as follows:

- Private: A private member within a class denotes that only members of the same class have accessibility. The private member is not accessible from outside the class.

- Public: The members declared as public are accessible from outside the class through an object of the class.

- Protected: A protected access specifier is a stage between private and public access. If member functions defined in a class are protected, they cannot be accessed from outside the class but can be accessed from the derived class (inheritance). The members declared as Protected are accessible from outside the class but only in a class derived from it.

Example:

```
class item

{

int number; // variables declaration

float cost; // private by default

public:

void getdata(int a, float b);// functions declaration

void putdata(void); //using prototype
```

It can be represented in the figure as follows:

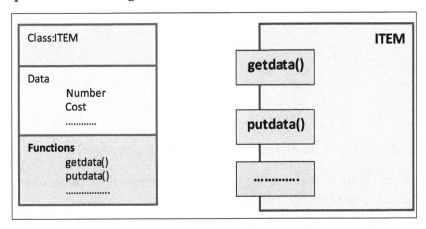

## Main C++ Program Function Called Main ( )

The main function is where a program starts execution. In C++, main() returns an integer value to the operating system. Every main() in C++ program should end with a return(o) statement, otherwise, a warning or an error may occur. Since, main() return an integer type value, it is must that return type of the main() must be explicitly specified as int. that return type of the main() must be explicitly specified as int.

Syntax: `int main ( )`

## Beginning of the Main Program: Left Brace {

The beginning of the main program can be specified by using left curly brace "{" . It consists of:

- Object declaration part

- Accessing member functions (using dot operator)

## Object Declaration Part

The objects of class can be declared inside the main program or outside the main program. A class declaration is used only to build the structure of an object. The data members and member functions are combined in the class. The declaration of objects is same as declaration of variables of basic data types. Defining objects of class data type is known as class instantiation (instances of class). In C++, the class variables are known as objects. When the objects are created, then memory is allocated to them. Any number of objects can be created for a particular given class. Objects can also be created when a class is defined by placing their names immediately after the closing brace, as it is done in the structure.

Example:

```
Circle c1;

//c1 is the object of class Circle
```

Example:

```
item x; // memory for x is created.

item x, y, z;
```

## Accessing Member Functions (Using Dot Operator)

The member functions defined in the class can be accessed by using dot (.) operator.
Syntax: object1.member function();

Example: c1.read();

In the above example, c1 is object of class circle and read() is the member function of class circle and operator dot (.) is used to access member functions.

## Ending of The Main Program: Right Brace }

The ending of the main program can be specified by using right curly brace "}".

## Input Operator

The identifier cin is a predefined object in C++ that corresponds to the standard input stream. The standard input stream represents the keyboard. The operator >> is known as extraction or get from operator. It extracts or takes the value from the keyboard and assigns it to the variable on its right.

Example:

```
cin>>number1;
```

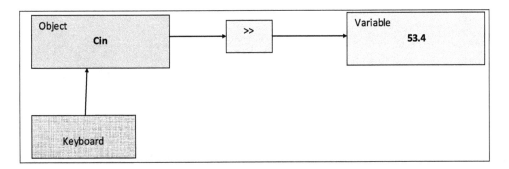

The above statement causes the program to wait for the user to type in a number. The number keyed in is placed in the variable number.

Program to implement the usage of input operator:

```
#include<iostream>

using namespace std;

int main()

{

cin>>a;

return 0;

}
```

## Output Operator

The identifier cout is a predefined object that represents the standard output stream in C++. The standard output stream represents the screen. It is also possible to redirect the output to other output devices. The operator << is called the insertion or put to operator. It extracts (or takes) the value from the keyboard and assigns it to the variable on its right.

**Example:**  `cout<< "c++ is better than c \n";`

Program to implement the usage of output operator:

```
#include<iostream>

using namespace std;

int main()

{

cout<<" c++ is better than c \n";
```

```
return 0;

}
```

When the above code is compiled and executed, it produces the following result: c++ is better than c. **Program to accept the name and display the name on the screen:**

```
#include <iostream>

using namespace std;

int main ( )

{

        char name[50];

        cout << "Please enter name:\n ";

        cin >> name;

        cout << "Name is: " << name << "\n";

}
```

When the above code is compiled and executed, it produces the following result:

> Please enter name
>
> xyz
>
> Name is xyz

**Program to implement the usage of input and output operators:**

```
#include<iostream>

using namespace std;

int main()

{

int a,b;

cout<<"enter the value of variable a \n";

cin>>a;

cout<<"enter the value of variable b \n";

cin>>b;
```

```
cout<<"value of variable a is "<<a<<"\n";

cout<<"vaue of variable b is "

return 0;

}
```

When the above code is compiled and executed, it produces the following result:

enter the value of variable a

10

enter the value of variable b

20

value of variable a is 10

value of variable a is 20

Program to enter an integer value and print its value and its value when it is doubled:

```
#include <iostream>

using namespace std;

int main ()

{

    int i;

    cout << "Please enter an integer value: \n ";

    cin >> i;

    cout << "The value you entered is " << i;

    cout << " and its double is " << i*2 << ".\n";

    return 0;

}
```

When the above code is compiled and executed, it produces the following result:

Please enter an integer value-

5

The value you entered is 5 and its double is 10

## Cascading of I/O Operators

The multiple use of << or >> in one statement is called cascading. When cascading an output operator, it is must to ensure that necessary blank spaces appears between different items. The output operator can be combined using the cascading technique as follows:

**Example:** `cout << "Sum = " << sum << "\n" << "Average = " << average << "\n";`

The input operator can also be cascaded as follows:

**Example:** `cin >> number1 >> number2;`

Program to implement the usage of cascading of Input operator:

```cpp
#include<iostream>

using namespace std;

int main()

{

int rno;

float total;

cout<<"enter the rno and total marks\n";

cin>>rno>>total;

cout<<"Rno is "<<rno<<"\n";

cout<<"Total marks is "<<total<<"\n";

return 0;

}
```

When the above code is compiled and executed, it produces the following result:

> enter the rno
>
> 10
>
> enter the total marks
>
> 450
>
> Rno is 10
>
> Total marks is 450

Program to implement the usage of cascading of Output operator:

```
#include<iostream>

using namespace std;

int main()

{

int testno;

float total;

cout<<"enter the testno\n";

cin>>testno;

cout<<"enter the total\n";

cin>>total;

cout<<"testno is "<<testno<<"total is "<<total<<"\n";

return 0;

}
```

When the above code is compiled and executed, it produces the following result:

enter the testno

101

enter the total

450

testno is 101

total is 450

Program to implement the usage of cascading of Input/Output operator to calculate area of rectangle:

```
#include<iostream>

using namespace std;

int main()

{
```

```
float length, breadth,area;

cout<<"enter the length and breadth\n";

cin>>length>>breadth;

area = length * breadth;

cout<<"Length is "<<length<<" Breadth is "<<breadth<<" Area
is"<<area<<"\n";

return 0;

}
```

When the above code is compiled and executed, it produces the following result:

> enter the length and breadth
>
> 10.5 12.5
>
> Length is 10.5 Breadth is 12.5 Area is 131.25

Program to accept Empno, Name of the Employee, Salary of the Employee and display the details on the screen:

```
#include<iostream>

using namespace std;

int main()

{

int eno;

char ename[30];

float salary;

cout<<"enter the employee no \n";

cin>>eno;

cout<<"enter the employee name\n";

cin>>ename;

cout<<"enter the salary of the employee\n";

cin>>salary;
```

```
cout<<"Employee no is "<<eno<<"\n";

cout<<"Employee Name is "<<ename<<"\n";

cout<<"Employee Salary is "<<salary<<"\n";

return 0;

}
```

When the above code is compiled and executed, it produces the following result:

enter the employee no

101

enter the employee name

hook

enter the salary of the employee

12000

Employee no is 101

Employee Name is hook

Employee Salary is 12000

Program to implement the usage of class:

```
// Header Files

#include <iostream>

using namespace std;

// Class Declaration

class person

{

//Access - Specifier

public:

        //Variable Declaration

        char name[80];

        int number;

};
```

```
//Main Function

int main()

{

    // Object Creation For Class

    person p1;

    //Get Input Values For Object Varibales

    cout<<"Enter the Name :";

    cin>>p1.name;

    cout<<"Enter the Number :";

    cin>>p1.number;

    //Show the Output

    cout << "Name is "<<p1.name << ": " << "Number is "<<p1.number
    << "\n";

    return 0;

}
```

When the above code is compiled and executed, it produces the following result:

> Enter the Name
>
> Deepali
>
> Enter the number
>
> 101
>
> Name is Deepali : Number is 101

**Program to find the area of circle using basic structure of C++ program with classes:**

```
// Program to find the area of circle using basic structure of C++ program

//Preprocessor Directives: Link and Definition Section

#include <iostream.h> // Link Section

#include <conio.h> // Link Section

#define PI 3.142 // Definition Section

//Global Declaration Section

    float r;
```

```
//Class declaration or definition

     class Circle

     {

     private:

     float area;

     public:

     void read()

     {

     cout<<"Enter the radius of the circle\n";

     cin>>r;

     }

     void display()

     {

     area = PI * r*r;

     cout<< "Area of circle is " <<area<<"\n";

     }

     };

//Main program starts

     int main ( )

//Beginning of the main program: Left brace

       {

     circle c1;

     c1.read();

     c1.display();

     return ();

//Ending of the main program: Right brace

   }
```

When the above code is compiled and executed, it produces the following result:

Enter the radius of the circle

7

Area of circle is 153.958

## Creation of Source file

On the operating systems like UNIX or LINUX, vi or ed text editor is used for creating using any text editor for creating and editing the source code. Turbo C++ provides an integrated environment for developing and editing programs. The file name should have a proper file extension to indicate that it is a C++ implementations, such as .cc, .cpp and .cxx. Turbo C++ and Borland C++ use .cpp(C plus plus) for C++ programs.

## Compiling and Linking

The process of compiling and linking again depends upon the operating system. Under LINUX operating system, the "g++" command is used to compile the program.

Example: At the LINUX prompt, suppose, if the C++ program source code is contained in the file "example.cpp". Then the compiler would produce an object file example.o and then automatically link with the library functions to produce an executable file. The default executable filename is a. out in LINUX operating system. Turbo C++ and Borland C++ provide an integrated program development environment under MS DOS.

## Scope Resolution Operator

Like C, C++ is also a block structured programming language. Blocks and scope can be used in constructing programs. Same variable name can be used to have different meanings in different blocks. In C language , global version of a variable cannot be accessed from within the inner block, but in C++ this problem can be resolved by introducing a new operator :: called scope resolution operator, which is used to uncover a hidden variable. The scope resolution operator allows access to global version of the variable and not the local variable declared in that block.

It takes the form as follows:

:: variable-name

Example:

```
#include <iostream>

int n = 12; // A global variable
```

```
int main()

{

int n = 13; // A local variable

cout << ::n << '\n'; // Print the global variable: 12

::cout << n << '\n'; // Print the local variable: 13

}
```

When the above code is compiled and executed, it produces the following result:

12

13

## This Pointer

This pointer is a special pointer which is built-in pointer. C++ uses a unique keyword called this to represent an object that invokes a member function. It stores the address of current object in context. The current object can be referred using this pointer anywhere in the class. "this" is a pointer that points to the object for which this function is called. this pointer can be used only inside the class, i.e. only inside the member function of the class and cannot be used outside the class. this pointer is a constant pointer. The unique this pointer is automatically passed to a member function when it is called. This pointer acts as an implicit argument to all the member functions. When non-static member"s function is called for an object, the address of the object is passed as hidden argument to the function.

Example: Suppose the function call is as follows:

```
mydate.setmonth(3);
```

It is interpreted as:

```
setmonth(&mydate, 3);
```

## Features of this Pointer

- It is an implicit pointer used by the system.
- It stores the address of the current object in reference.
- It is constant pointer to an object.
- The object pointed to by the „this" pointer can be dereferenced and modified.
- It can only be used within non-static functions of the class.
- This pointer is non-modifiable, assignment to this are not allowed.

**Program to implement the usage of this pointer:**

```cpp
#include<iostream>

class Test

{

private:

int x;

public:

void setX (int x)     .

{

this->x = x;

}

void print()

{

cout << "x = "<< x << endl;

}

};

int main()

{

Test obj;

int x =20;

obj.setX(x);

obj.print();

return 0;

}
```

When the above code is compiled and executed, it produces the following result:

        x=20

# Elements and Features of C++ Programming Language

There are several basic elements and features of C++ programming language such as syntax, comments, complier, variables, storage class, operator and expressions, and data types. Syntax is the set of rules which ensures that the combinations of symbols are correctly structured. All these diverse elements and features of C++ programming language have been carefully analyzed in this chapter.

## Syntax

The term "Syntax" is a set of pre-defined protocols or rules that we need to follow in a programming language. Every programming language has its own unique syntax. Similarly, C++ Syntax also has its significance.

### Basic C++ Syntax

The expression "Syntax" refers to the rules that we need to strictly follow while writing a program. In order to get an error-free output, we diligently need to follow these pre-defined rules. In order to develop a clear and concise understanding of the C++ syntax, let us take the "Hello world!" program into consideration. This is the simplest program you can make in C++.

Here is a C++ program to print "Hello world!" on the output screen:

```
#include<iostream>

using namespace std;


/* This is my first C++ program */


int main()

{

cout<<"Hello world!"<<endl;
```

```
return 0;

}
```

## Code

## Output

From the above program, you might have got a basic idea about the syntax and structure of a C++ program, how the elements of the program are placed together and how we get the output on the display screen.

## Components of the C++ Program

From the above program, it is pretty clear that there are various components in a C++ program which includes header files, the main function and the body of the program.

## Header Files

**#include<iostream>**

In this header file, 'iostream' stands for the input-output stream.

In general, a header file instructs the C++ compiler to include all the functions associated with that header file. Here, the <iostream> header file allows you to use the input and output operations. We have performed an output operation of displaying the message "Hello world!" on the screen with the help of the cout function.

## Namespace

Namespace refers to the declarative region that gives scope to all the identifiers (a unique name given to variables and functions according to a set of rules) used inside it.

In the "Hello world!" program, we have written a statement:

```
using namespace std;
```

The above statement is written in every C++ program. It is a relatively new concept introduced by the latest C standards. This statement basically instructs the C++ compiler to use the standard namespace. Another way of using namespace is by the use of the scope resolution operator "::" This is how we will use it:

```
std::cout<<"Hello world!";
```

It instructs the compiler that every time you write cout, you are referring to std::cout

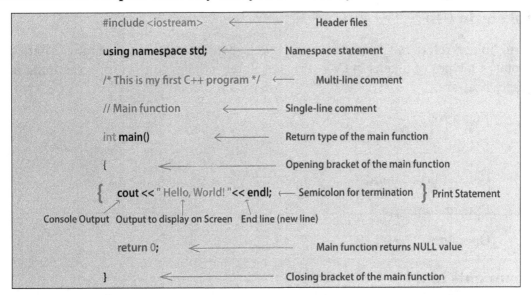

## The Main Function

Every C++ program necessarily contains at least one function, that is, the main function. Every statement in C++ executes line by line in the main function. According to the latest C++ Standards, it is necessary to specify the return type of the main function as int.

## {AND}

The curly braces '{' and '}' denote the opening and closing of a statement respectively. In the "Hello world!" program, the opening and closing braces denote the start and end of the main function.

## Print Statement

In order to print or display a message on the screen, use the 'cout' function. The 'cout' function is followed by the output operator '<<' followed by the text to be printed enclosed within double quotes. It is similar to the printf() function in C except for the fact we do not require format specifiers.

```
cout<<"Hello world!"<<endl;
```

Here, the endl statement stands for the end of the line. It instructs the compiler to move to the new line. It is similar to the '\n' escape sequence.

## Return 0

The return 0 statement signifies that the main function would return a null value.

## Tokens in C++

Term 'token' refers to the smallest possible individual unit in a program. There are a total of 5 types of tokens in C++. It is absolutely similar to the C programming language. They are:

- Keywords
- Identifiers
- Constants or Literals
- Punctuators
- Operators

## Comments in C++

Comments in C++ are statements that are not executable when the program is run. They are simply used for the user's convenience. There are 2 types of comments in C++:

- Single line comments: Anything written b=after '//' operator is considered as a single-line comment.

For instance,

```
// Welcome to DataFlair tutorials!
```

- Multi-line comments: Anything written within '/*' and '*/' is considered as a multi-line comment.

For instance,

```
/* Welcome to DataFlair tutorials!

We Hope you enjoy our tutorials! */
```

In the "Hello World" program, We have used a multi-line comment.

```
/* This is my first C++ program */
```

## Whitespaces in C++

White spaces are nothing but blank spaces. Whitespaces separate elements of a program from one another.

For instance, In the statement,

```
int value;
```

If you don't separate int and value with whitespace then the statement would make no sense and you would get a compilation error.

## Semicolons in C++

We use semicolons in C++ to indicate the termination of a statement. If they are not used as and when required, you would get a compilation error.

## Basic Rules for Writing C++ Program

C++ is a case sensitive language. Therefore, uppercase and lowercase characters are treated differently. It must be kept in mind while coding in C++. Most of the keywords in C++ are in lowercase. All statements must necessarily terminate with a semicolon. Whitespace should be provided duly between keywords and variables in C/C++.

# Comments

The C++ comments are statements that are not executed by the compiler. The comments in C++ programming can be used to provide explanation of the code, variable, method or class. By the help of comments, you can hide the program code also.

There are two types of comments in C++:

- Single Line comment
- Multi Line comment

## C++ Single Line Comment

The single line comment starts with // (double slash). Let's see an example of single line comment in C++.

```cpp
#include <iostream>

using namespace std;

int main()

{

 int x = 11; // x is a variable

 cout<<x<<"\n";

}
```

Output: 11

## C++ Multi Line Comment

The C++ multi line comment is used to comment multiple lines of code. It is surrounded by slash and asterisk (/* ..... */). Let's see an example of multi-line comment in C++:

```cpp
#include <ostream>

using namespace std;

int main()

{

/* declare and

print variable in C++. */

 int x = 35;

 cout<<x<<"\n";

}
```

Output: 35

# Compiler

Compilers are utility programs that take your code and transform it into executable machine code files. When you run a compiler on your code, first, the preprocessor reads the source code (the C++ file you just wrote). The preprocessor searches for any preprocessor directives (lines of code starting with a #). Preprocessor directives cause the preprocessor to change your code in some way (by usually adding some library or another C++ file).

Next, the compiler works through the preprocessed code line by line translating each line into the appropriate machine language instruction. This will also uncover any syntax errors that are present in your source code and will throw an error to the command line.

Finally, if no errors are present, the compiler creates an object file with the machine language binary necessary to run on your machine. While the object file that the compiler just created is likely enough to do something on your computer, it still isn't a working executable of your C++ program. There is a final important step to reach an executable program.

C++ contains a vast library to aid in performing difficult tasks like I/O and hardware manipulation. You can include these libraries with preprocessor directives, but the preprocessor doesn't automatically add them to your code. In order for you to have a final executable program, another utility known as the linker must combine your object files with the library functions necessary to run the code.

Think of it as having all the necessary blocks to build a house. The compiler made all the blocks but the linker is the one that sticks them all together to finally create a house. Once this is done, you now have a functioning executable file.

## How to Compile a File

## If you are on Windows

- Using and IDE like CodeBlocks: It is as simple as clicking the build and run buttons, they will create a file in the project folder.

- Using Command Prompt.

- Open a Developer Command Prompt - For this step, you will need to have Microsoft Visual Studio or some other IDE that enables you to compile your program from the command line. You can also search online for C++ compilers.

- Navigate to the source code directly.

- Run the Compiler on your source code. (assuming you are using the Microsoft Visual Studio compiler) `cl /EHsc helloWorld.cpp`

This will now create an object file and automatically link it for you. If you look in that same folder, you will see a hellWorld.exe executable file (note the exe extension) is now present.

- Type hello World into the prompt to run the executable.

Alternatively, many IDEs allow for quick building and viewing of your program. This may be easier since your version of windows may not come prepackaged with a compiler utility.

### If you are on Linux or OSX

- Open up a terminal window and navigate to the source code directory.

- Run the Compiler on your source code `g++ helloWorld.cpp -o helloWorld`

This will create an object file and automatically link it for you. Look in the folder and you will see a helloWorld.exe executable file (note the exe extension).

- Type `./helloWorld` in the terminal window to run the executable file.

g++ is the standard Linux compiler and is a great utility. It comes packaged with the operating system.

To compile and execute your code directly, run `g++ -o helloWorld helloWorld.cpp; ./helloWorld` so when you need to compile and run your code multiple times, up arrow-enter. There are a number of different types of compilers. The two listed are the two that are usually packaged with Windows or Linux/OSX.

## Variables

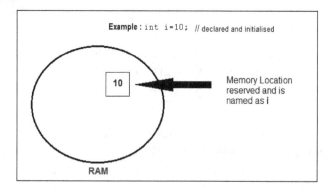

Variable are used in C++, where we need storage for any value, which will change in program. Variable can be declared in multiple ways each with different memory requirements and functioning. Variable is the name of memory location allocated by the compiler depending upon the data_type of the variable.

## Basic Types of Variables

Each variable while declaration must be given a datatype, on which the memory assigned to the variable depends. Following are the basic types of variables,

| | |
|---|---|
| bool | For variable to store boolean values( True or False ) |
| char | For variables to store character types. |
| int | for variable with integral values |
| float and double are also types for variables with large and floating point values | |

## How to Declare variables?

A typical variable declaration is of the form:

```
// Declaring a single variable

type variable_name;
```

```
// Declaring multiple variables:

type variable1_name, variable2_name, variable3_name;
```

A variable name can consist of alphabets (both upper and lower case), numbers and the underscore '_' character. However, the name must not start with a number.

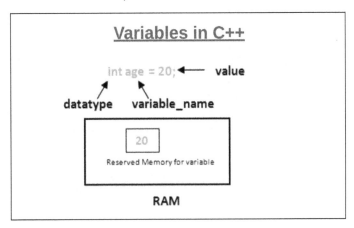

In the above diagram,

      datatype: Type of data that can be stored in this variable.

      variable_name: Name given to the variable.

      value: It is the initial value stored in the variable.

**Examples:**

```
// Declaring float variable

float simpleInterest;


// Declaring integer variable

int time, speed;


// Declaring character variable

char var;
```

## Difference between Variable Declaration and Definition

The variable declaration refers to the part where a variable is first declared or introduced before its first use. A variable definition is a part where the variable is assigned a memory location and a value. Most of the times, variable declaration and definition are done together.

```
#include <iostream>

using namespace std;


int main()

{

    // declaration and definition

    // of variable <a123>

    char a123 = 'a';


    // This is also both declaration and definition

    // as <b> is allocated memory and

    // assigned some garbage value.

    float b;
```

```
    // multiple declarations and definitions

    int _c, _d45, e;


    // Let us print a variable

    cout << a123 << endl;


    return 0;

}
```

Output: a

There are three types of variables based on the scope of variables in C++:

- Local Variables
- Instance Variables
- Static Variables

- Local Variables: A variable defined within a block or method or constructor is called local variable.
  - These variable are created when the block in entered or the function is called and destroyed after exiting from the block or when the call returns from the function.

○   The scope of these variables exists only within the block in which the variable is declared. i.e. we can access these variable only within that block.

○   Initilisation of Local Variable is Mandatory.

**Sample Program:**

```cpp
// C++ program to demonstrate Local variables


#include <iostream>
using namespace std;


void StudentAge()
{
    // local variable age
    int age = 0;
    age = age + 5;
    cout << "Student age is : " << age;
}


// Driver code
int main()
{
    StudentAge();
}
```

**Output:** Student age is : 5

In the above program, the variable age is a local variable to the function StudentAge(). If we use the variable age outside StudentAge() function, the compiler will produce an error as shown in below program.

**Sample Program:**

```cpp
// C++ program to demonstrate Local variables
```

```cpp
#include <iostream>
using namespace std;


void StudentAge()
{

    // local variable age

    int age = 0;

    age = age + 5;

}


// Driver code

int main()
{

    StudentAge();

    cout << "Student age is : " << age;

}
```

- **Instance Variables:** Instance variables are non-static variables and are declared in a class outside any method, constructor or block.

  ○ As instance variables are declared in a class, these variables are created when an object of the class is created and destroyed when the object is destroyed.

  ○ Unlike local variables, we may use access specifiers for instance variables. If we do not specify any access specifier then the default access specifier will be used.

  ○ Initilisation of Instance Variable is not Mandatory.

  ○ Instance Variable can be accessed only by creating objects.

**Sample Program:**

```cpp
// C++ program to demonstrate Local variables
```

```cpp
#include <iostream>

using namespace std;


class Marks {


public:

    // This is a class variable

    static int studentNumber;


    // These variables are instance variables.

    // These variables are in a class

    // and are not inside any function

    int engMarks;

    int mathsMarks;

    int phyMarks;


public:

    Marks()

    {


        // Modify the class variable

        ++studentNumber;

    };

};


// Setting the class variable of Marks
```

```cpp
int Marks::studentNumber = 0;


// Driver code
int main()
{

    // first object
    Marks obj1;
    obj1.engMarks = 50;
    obj1.mathsMarks = 80;
    obj1.phyMarks = 90;


    // second object
    Marks obj2;
    obj2.engMarks = 80;
    obj2.mathsMarks = 60;
    obj2.phyMarks = 85;


    // displaying marks for first object
    cout << "Marks for first object:\n";
    cout << Marks::studentNumber << endl;
    cout << obj1.engMarks << endl;
    cout << obj1.mathsMarks << endl;
    cout << obj1.phyMarks << endl;


    // displaying marks for second object
```

```
    cout << "Marks for second object:\n";

    cout << Marks::studentNumber << endl;

    cout << obj2.engMarks << endl;

    cout << obj2.mathsMarks << endl;

    cout << obj2.phyMarks << endl;

}
```

Output:

Marks for first object:

2

50

80

90

Marks for second object:

2

80

60

85

As you can see in the above program the variables, engMarks , mathsMarks , phy-Marks are instance variables. In case we have multiple objects as in the above program, each object will have its own copies of instance variables. It is clear from the above output that each object will have its own copy of instance variable.

- Static Variables: Static variables are also known as Class variables.

  ○ These variables are declared similarly as instance variables, the difference is that static variables are declared using the static keyword within a class outside any method constructor or block.

  ○ Unlike instance variables, we can only have one copy of a static variable per class irrespective of how many objects we create.

  ○ Static variables are created at the start of program execution and destroyed automatically when execution ends.

- ○   Initialization of Static Variable is not Mandatory. Its default value is 0.

- ○   If we access the static variable like Instance variable (through an object), the compiler will show the warning message and it won't halt the program. The compiler will replace the object name to class name automatically.

- ○   If we access the static variable without the class name, Compiler will automatically append the class name.

To access static variables, we need not create an object of that class, we can simply access the variable as:

```
class_name::variable_name;
```

**Sample Program:**

```cpp
// C++ program to demonstrate Static variables


#include <iostream>

using namespace std;


class Marks {


public:

    // This is a class variable

    static int studentNumber;


    // These variables are instance variables.

    // These variables are in a class

    // and are not inside any function

    int engMarks;

    int mathsMarks;

    int phyMarks;
```

```
    Marks()

    {


        // Modify the class variable

        ++studentNumber;

    };

};


// Setting the class variable of Marks

int Marks::studentNumber = 0;


// Driver code

int main()

{


    // object of Marks

    Marks obj1;

    obj1.engMarks = 50;

    obj1.mathsMarks = 80;

    obj1.phyMarks = 90;


    // displaying marks for first object

    cout << "Marks for object:\n";

    // Now to display the static variable,

    // it can be directly done

    // using the class name
```

```
    cout << Marks::studentNumber << endl;

    // But same is not the case

    // with instance variables

    cout << obj1.engMarks << endl;

    cout << obj1.mathsMarks << endl;

    cout << obj1.phyMarks << endl;

}
```

Output:

> Marks for object:
>
> 1
>
> 50
>
> 80
>
> 90

## Instance Variable Vs Static Variable

- Each object will have its own copy of instance variable whereas We can only have one copy of a static variable per class irrespective of how many objects we create.

- Changes made in an instance variable using one object will not be reflected in other objects as each object has its own copy of instance variable. In case of static, changes will be reflected in other objects as static variables are common to all object of a class.

- We can access instance variables through object references and Static Variables can be accessed directly using class name.

Syntax for static and instance variables:

```
class Example

{

    static int a; // static variable

    int b;        // instance variable

}
```

## Storage Class

A storage class defines the scope (visibility) and life-time of variables and/or functions within a C++ Program. These specifiers precede the type that they modify. There are following storage classes, which can be used in a C++ Program.

- auto
- register
- static
- extern
- mutable

### The Auto Storage Class

The auto storage class is the default storage class for all local variables.

```
{
    int mount;

    auto int month;
}
```

The example above defines two variables with the same storage class, auto can only be used within functions, i.e., local variables.

### The Register Storage Class

The register storage class is used to define local variables that should be stored in a register instead of RAM. This means that the variable has a maximum size equal to the register size (usually one word) and can't have the unary '&' operator applied to it (as it does not have a memory location).

```
{
    register int  miles;
}
```

The register should only be used for variables that require quick access such as counters. It should also be noted that defining 'register' does not mean that the variable will be stored in a register. It means that it MIGHT be stored in a register depending on hardware and implementation restrictions.

## The Static Storage Class

The static storage class instructs the compiler to keep a local variable in existence during the life-time of the program instead of creating and destroying it each time it comes into and goes out of scope. Therefore, making local variables static allows them to maintain their values between function calls.

The static modifier may also be applied to global variables. When this is done, it causes that variable's scope to be restricted to the file in which it is declared. In C++, when static is used on a class data member, it causes only one copy of that member to be shared by all objects of its class.

```cpp
#include <iostream>


// Function declaration

void func(void);


static int count = 10; /* Global variable */


main() {

    while(count--) {

        func();

    }


    return 0;

}


// Function definition

void func( void ) {

    static int i = 5; // local static variable

    i++;

    std::cout << "i is " << i ;
```

```
    std::cout << " and count is " << count << std::endl;
}
```

When the above code is compiled and executed, it produces the following result:

```
i is 6 and count is 9

i is 7 and count is 8

i is 8 and count is 7

i is 9 and count is 6

i is 10 and count is 5

i is 11 and count is 4

i is 12 and count is 3

i is 13 and count is 2

i is 14 and count is 1

i is 15 and count is 0
```

## The Extern Storage Class

The extern storage class is used to give a reference of a global variable that is visible to ALL the program files. When you use 'extern' the variable cannot be initialized as all it does is point the variable name at a storage location that has been previously defined.

When you have multiple files and you define a global variable or function, which will be used in other files also, then extern will be used in another file to give reference of defined variable or function. Just for understanding extern is used to declare a global variable or function in another file. The extern modifier is most commonly used when there are two or more files sharing the same global variables or functions as explained below.

First File: main.cpp

```
#include <iostream>

int count ;

extern void write_extern();


main() {
```

```
    count = 5;

    write_extern();

}
```

**Second File:** `support.cpp`

```cpp
#include <iostream>


extern int count;


void write_extern(void) {

    std::cout << "Count is " << count << std::endl;

}
```

Here, extern keyword is being used to declare count in another file. Now compile these two files as follows:

```
$g++ main.cpp support.cpp -o write
```

This will produce write executable program, try to execute write and check the result as follows:

```
$./write
5
```

## The Mutable Storage Class

The mutable specifier applies only to class objects, which are discussed later in this tutorial. It allows a member of an object to override const member function. That is, a mutable member can be modified by a const member function.

# Allied Aspects of C++ Programming Language

Some of the aspects related to C++ programming language are generic programming, metaprogramming, C++ standard library, C++ string handling. In generic programming, general algorithms are written which work with all data types. This chapter has been carefully written to provide an easy understanding of the varied facets of C++ programming language.

## Generic Programming

In the simplest definition, generic programming is a style of computer programming in which algorithms are written in terms of types *to-be-specified-later* that are then *instantiated* when needed for specific types provided as parameters. This approach, pioneered by ML in 1973, permits writing common functions or types that differ only in the set of types on which they operate when used, thus reducing duplication. Such software entities are known as *generics* in Ada, Delphi, Eiffel, Java, C#, F#, Objective-C, Swift, and Visual Basic .NET; *parametric polymorphism* in ML, Scala, Haskell (the Haskell community also uses the term "generic" for a related but somewhat different concept) and Julia; *templates* in C++ and D; and *parameterized types* in the influential 1994 book *Design Patterns*. The authors of *Design Patterns* note that this technique, especially when combined with delegation, is very powerful but also quote the following:

Dynamic, highly parameterized software is harder to understand than more static software.

*—Gang of Four, Design Patterns (Chapter 1)*

The term generic programming was originally coined by David Musser and Alexander Stepanov in a more specific sense than the above, to describe a programming paradigm whereby fundamental requirements on types are abstracted from across concrete examples of algorithms and data structures and formalised as concepts, with generic functions implemented in terms of these concepts, typically using language genericity mechanisms as described above.

### Stepanov–Musser and Other Generic Programming Paradigms

Generic programming is defined in Musser & Stepanov (1989) as follows,

Generic programming centers around the idea of abstracting from concrete, efficient algorithms to obtain generic algorithms that can be combined with different data representations to produce a wide variety of useful software.

*— Musser, David R.; Stepanov, Alexander A., Generic Programming*

Generic programming paradigm is an approach to software decomposition whereby fundamental requirements on types are abstracted from across concrete examples of algorithms and data structures and formalised as concepts, analogously to the abstraction of algebraic theories in abstract algebra. Early examples of this programming approach were implemented in Scheme and Ada, although the best known example is the Standard Template Library (STL), which developed a theory of iterators that is used to decouple sequence data structures and the algorithms operating on them.

For example, given $N$ sequence data structures, e.g. singly linked list, vector etc., and $M$ algorithms to operate on them, e.g. find, sort etc., a direct approach would implement each algorithm specifically for each data structure, giving $N \times M$ combinations to implement. However, in the generic programming approach, each data structure returns a model of an iterator concept (a simple value type which can be dereferenced to retrieve the current value, or changed to point to another value in the sequence) and each algorithm is instead written generically with arguments of such iterators, e.g. a pair of iterators pointing to the beginning and end of the subsequence to process. Thus, only $N + M$ data structure-algorithm combinations need be implemented. Several iterator concepts are specified in the STL, each a refinement of more restrictive concepts e.g. forward iterators only provide movement to the next value in a sequence (e.g. suitable for a singly linked list or a stream of input data), whereas a random-access iterator also provides direct constant-time access to any element of the sequence (e.g. suitable for a vector). An important point is that a data structure will return a model of the most general concept that can be implemented efficiently—computational complexity requirements are explicitly part of the concept definition. This limits which data structures a given algorithm can be applied to and such complexity requirements are a major determinant of data structure choice. Generic programming similarly has been applied in other domains, e.g. graph algorithms.

Note that although this approach often utilizes language features of compile-time genericity/templates, it is in fact independent of particular language-technical details. Generic programming pioneer Alexander Stepanov wrote,

Generic programming is about abstracting and classifying algorithms and data structures. It gets its inspiration from Knuth and not from type theory. Its goal is the incremental construction of systematic catalogs of useful, efficient and abstract algorithms and data structures. Such an undertaking is still a dream.

*— Alexander Stepanov, Short History of STL*

I believe that iterator theories are as central to Computer Science as theories of rings or Banach spaces are central to Mathematics.

*—Alexander Stepanov, An Interview with A. Stepanov*

Bjarne Stroustrup noted,

Following Stepanov, we can define generic programming without mentioning language features: Lift algorithms and data structures from concrete examples to their most general and abstract form.

*—Bjarne Stroustrup, Evolving a language in*
*and for the real world: C++ 1991-2006*

Other programming paradigms that have been described as generic programming include *Datatype generic programming* as described in "Generic Programming — an Introduction". The *Scrap your boilerplate* approach is a lightweight generic programming approach for Haskell.

In this article we distinguish the high-level programming paradigms of *generic programming*, above, from the lower-level programming language *genericity mechanisms* used to implement them. For further discussion and comparison of generic programming paradigms.

## Programming Language Support for Genericity

Genericity facilities have existed in high-level languages since at least the 1970s in languages such as ML, CLU and Ada, and were subsequently adopted by many object-based and object-oriented languages, including BETA, C++, D, Eiffel, Java, and DEC's now defunct Trellis-Owl language.

Genericity is implemented and supported differently in various programming languages; the term "generic" has also been used differently in various programming contexts. For example, in Forth the compiler can execute code while compiling and one can create new *compiler keywords* and new implementations for those words on the fly. It has few *words* that expose the compiler behaviour and therefore naturally offers *genericity* capacities which, however, are not referred to as such in most Forth texts. Similarly, dynamically typed languages, especially interpreted ones, usually offer *genericity* by default as both passing values to functions and value assignment are type-indifferent and such behavior is often utilized for abstraction or code terseness, however this is not typically labeled *genericity* as it's a direct consequence of dynamic typing system employed by the language. The term has been used in functional programming, specifically in Haskell-like languages, which use a structural type system where types are always parametric and the actual code on those types is generic. These usages still serve a similar purpose of code-saving and the rendering of an abstraction.

Arrays and structs can be viewed as predefined generic types. Every usage of an array or struct type instantiates a new concrete type, or reuses a previous instantiated type. Array element types and struct element types are parameterized types, which are used to instantiate the corresponding generic type. All this is usually built-in in the compiler and the syntax differs from other generic constructs. Some extensible programming languages try to unify built-in and user defined generic types.

A broad survey of genericity mechanisms in programming languages follows. For a specific survey comparing suitability of mechanisms for generic programming.

## In Object-oriented Languages

When creating container classes in statically typed languages, it is inconvenient to write specific implementations for each datatype contained, especially if the code for each datatype is virtually identical. For example, in C++, this duplication of code can be circumvented by defining a class template:

```
template<typename T>

class List

{

    /* class contents */

};



List<Animal> list_of_animals;

List<Car> list_of_cars;
```

Above, T is a placeholder for whatever type is specified when the list is created. These "containers-of-type-T", commonly called templates, allow a class to be reused with different datatypes as long as certain contracts such as subtypes and signature are kept. This genericity mechanism should not be confused with *inclusion polymorphism*, which is the algorithmic usage of exchangeable sub-classes: for instance, a list of objects of type Moving_Object containing objects of type Animal and Car. Templates can also be used for type-independent functions as in the Swap example below:

```
template<typename T>

void Swap(T & a, T & b) //"&" passes parameters by reference

{

    T temp = b;
```

```
   b = a;

   a = temp;

}
```


```
string hello = "world!", world = "Hello, ";

Swap( world, hello );

cout << hello << world << endl; //Output is "Hello, world!"
```

The C++ template construct used above is widely cited as the genericity construct that popularized the notion among programmers and language designers and supports many generic programming idioms. The D programming language also offers fully generic-capable templates based on the C++ precedent but with a simplified syntax. The Java programming language has provided genericity facilities syntactically based on C++'s since the introduction of J2SE 5.0.

C# 2.0, Chrome 1.5 and Visual Basic .NET 2005 have constructs that take advantage of the support for generics present in the Microsoft .NET Framework since version 2.0.

## Generics in Ada

Ada has had generics since it was first designed in 1977–1980. The standard library uses generics to provide many services. Ada 2005 adds a comprehensive generic container library to the standard library, which was inspired by C++'s standard template library.

A *generic unit* is a package or a subprogram that takes one or more *generic formal parameters*.

A *generic formal parameter* is a value, a variable, a constant, a type, a subprogram, or even an instance of another, designated, generic unit. For generic formal types, the syntax distinguishes between discrete, floating-point, fixed-point, access (pointer) types, etc. Some formal parameters can have default values.

To *instantiate* a generic unit, the programmer passes *actual* parameters for each formal. The generic instance then behaves just like any other unit. It is possible to instantiate generic units at run-time, for example inside a loop.

## Example

The specification of a generic package:

```
generic
```

```
    Max_Size : Natural; -- a generic formal value

    type Element_Type is private; -- a generic formal type; ac-
cepts any nonlimited type

 package Stacks is

    type Size_Type is range 0 .. Max_Size;

    type Stack is limited private;

    procedure Create (S : out Stack;

                         Initial_Size : in Size_Type := Max_Size);

     procedure Push (Into : in out Stack; Element : in Element_
Type);

     procedure Pop (From : in out Stack; Element : out Element_
Type);

    Overflow : exception;

    Underflow : exception;

 private

    subtype Index_Type is Size_Type range 1 .. Max_Size;

    type Vector is array (Index_Type range <>) of Element_Type;

    type Stack (Allocated_Size : Size_Type := 0) is record

       Top : Index_Type;

       Storage : Vector (1 .. Allocated_Size);

    end record;

 end Stacks;
```

Instantiating the generic package:

```
 type Bookmark_Type is new Natural;

 -- records a location in the text document we are editing


 package Bookmark_Stacks is new Stacks (Max_Size => 20,

                              Element_Type => Book-
```

```
mark_Type);

  -- Allows the user to jump between recorded locations in a doc-
ument

Using an instance of a generic package:

 type Document_Type is record

    Contents : Ada.Strings.Unbounded.Unbounded_String;

    Bookmarks : Bookmark_Stacks.Stack;

 end record;


 procedure Edit (Document_Name : in String) is

   Document : Document_Type;

 begin

   -- Initialise the stack of bookmarks:

   Bookmark_Stacks.Create (S => Document.Bookmarks, Initial_Size
=> 10);

   -- Now, open the file Document_Name and read it in...

 end Edit;
```

## Advantages and Limitations

The language syntax allows precise specification of constraints on generic formal parameters. For example, it is possible to specify that a generic formal type will only accept a modular type as the actual. It is also possible to express constraints *between* generic formal parameters; for example:

```
generic
    type Index_Type is (<>); -- must be a discrete type
    type Element_Type is private; -- can be any nonlimited type
    type Array_Type is array (Index_Type range <>) of Element_
Type;
```

In this example, Array_Type is constrained by both Index_Type and Element_Type. When instantiating the unit, the programmer must pass an actual array type that satisfies these constraints.

The disadvantage of this fine-grained control is a complicated syntax, but, because all generic formal parameters are completely defined in the specification, the compiler can instantiate generics without looking at the body of the generic.

Unlike C++, Ada does not allow specialised generic instances, and requires that all generics be instantiated explicitly. These rules have several consequences:

- The compiler can implement *shared generics*: the object code for a generic unit can be shared between all instances (unless the programmer requests inlining of subprograms, of course). As further consequences:

    o  There is no possibility of code bloat (code bloat is common in C++ and requires special care, as explained below).

    o  It is possible to instantiate generics at run-time, as well as at compile time, since no new object code is required for a new instance.

    o  Actual objects corresponding to a generic formal object are always considered to be nonstatic inside the generic.

- All instances of a generic being exactly the same, it is easier to review and understand programs written by others; there are no "special cases" to take into account.

- All instantiations being explicit, there are no hidden instantiations that might make it difficult to understand the program.

- Ada does not permit "template metaprogramming", because it does not allow specialisations.

## Templates in C++

C++ uses templates to enable generic programming techniques. The C++ Standard Library includes the Standard Template Library or STL that provides a framework of templates for common data structures and algorithms. Templates in C++ may also be used for template metaprogramming, which is a way of pre-evaluating some of the code at compile-time rather than run-time. Using template specialization, C++ Templates are considered Turing complete.

## Technical Overview

There are two kinds of templates: function templates and class templates. A *function template* is a pattern for creating ordinary functions based upon the parameterizing types supplied when instantiated. For example, the C++ Standard Template Library contains the function template max(x, y) which creates functions that return either *x* or *y*, whichever is larger. max() could be defined like this:

```
template <typename T>
```

```
T max(T x, T y)

{

    return x < y ? y : x;

}
```

*Specializations* of this function template, instantiations with specific types, can be called just like an ordinary function:

```
cout << max(3, 7);    // outputs 7
```

The compiler examines the arguments used to call max and determines that this is a call to max(int, int). It then instantiates a version of the function where the parameterizing type T is int, making the equivalent of the following function:

```
int max(int x, int y)

{

    return x < y ? y : x;

}
```

This works whether the arguments x and y are integers, strings, or any other type for which the expression x < y is sensible, or more specifically, for any type for which operator< is defined. Common inheritance is not needed for the set of types that can be used, and so it is very similar to duck typing. A program defining a custom data type can use operator overloading to define the meaning of < for that type, thus allowing its use with the max() function template. While this may seem a minor benefit in this isolated example, in the context of a comprehensive library like the STL it allows the programmer to get extensive functionality for a new data type, just by defining a few operators for it. Merely defining < allows a type to be used with the standard sort(), stable_sort(), and binary_search() algorithms or to be put inside data structures such as sets, heaps, and associative arrays.

C++ templates are completely type safe at compile time. As a demonstration, the standard type complex does not define the < operator, because there is no strict order on complex numbers. Therefore, max(x, y) will fail with a compile error if $x$ and $y$ are complex values. Likewise, other templates that rely on < cannot be applied to complex data unless a comparison (in the form of a functor or function) is provided. E.g.: A complex cannot be used as key for a map unless a comparison is provided. Unfortunately, compilers historically generate somewhat esoteric, long, and unhelpful error messages for this sort of error. Ensuring that a certain object adheres to a method protocol can alleviate this issue. Languages which use compare instead of < can also use complex values as keys.

The second kind of template, a *class template,* extends the same concept to classes. A class template specialization is a class. Class templates are often used to make generic containers. For example, the STL has a linked list container. To make a linked list of integers, one writes list<int>. A list of strings is denoted list<string>. A list has a set of standard functions associated with it, which work for any compatible parameterizing types.

## Template Specialization

A powerful feature of C++'s templates is *template specialization.* This allows alternative implementations to be provided based on certain characteristics of the parameterized type that is being instantiated. Template specialization has two purposes: to allow certain forms of optimization, and to reduce code bloat.

For example, consider a sort() template function. One of the primary activities that such a function does is to swap or exchange the values in two of the container's positions. If the values are large (in terms of the number of bytes it takes to store each of them), then it is often quicker to first build a separate list of pointers to the objects, sort those pointers, and then build the final sorted sequence. If the values are quite small however it is usually fastest to just swap the values in-place as needed. Furthermore, if the parameterized type is already of some pointer-type, then there is no need to build a separate pointer array. Template specialization allows the template creator to write different implementations and to specify the characteristics that the parameterized type(s) must have for each implementation to be used.

Unlike function templates, class templates can be partially specialized. That means that an alternate version of the class template code can be provided when some of the template parameters are known, while leaving other template parameters generic. This can be used, for example, to create a default implementation (the *primary specialization*) that assumes that copying a parameterizing type is expensive and then create partial specializations for types that are cheap to copy, thus increasing overall efficiency. Clients of such a class template just use specializations of it without needing to know whether the compiler used the primary specialization or some partial specialization in each case. Class templates can also be *fully specialized,* which means that an alternate implementation can be provided when all of the parameterizing types are known.

## Advantages and Disadvantages

Some uses of templates, such as the max() function, were previously filled by function-like preprocessor macros (a legacy of the C programming language). For example, here is a possible max() macro:

```
#define max(a,b) ((a) < (b) ? (b) : (a))
```

Macros are expanded by preprocessor, before compilation proper; templates are expanded at compile time. Macros are always expanded inline; templates can also be expanded as inline functions when the compiler deems it appropriate. Thus both function-like macros and function templates have no run-time overhead.

However, templates are generally considered an improvement over macros for these purposes. Templates are type-safe. Templates avoid some of the common errors found in code that makes heavy use of function-like macros, such as evaluating parameters with side effects twice. Perhaps most importantly, templates were designed to be applicable to much larger problems than macros.

There are three primary drawbacks to the use of templates: compiler support, poor error messages, and code bloat. Many compilers historically have poor support for templates, thus the use of templates can make code somewhat less portable. Support may also be poor when a C++ compiler is being used with a linker which is not C++-aware, or when attempting to use templates across shared library boundaries. Most modern compilers however now have fairly robust and standard template support, and the new C++ standard, C++11, further addresses these issues.

Almost all compilers produce confusing, long, or sometimes unhelpful error messages when errors are detected in code that uses templates. This can make templates difficult to develop.

Finally, the use of templates requires the compiler to generate a separate *instance* of the templated class or function for every permutation of type parameters used with it. (This is necessary because types in C++ are not all the same size, and the sizes of data fields are important to how classes work.) So the indiscriminate use of templates can lead to code bloat, resulting in excessively large executables. However, judicious use of template specialization and derivation can dramatically reduce such code bloat in some cases:

So, can derivation be used to reduce the problem of code replicated because templates are used? This would involve deriving a template from an ordinary class. This technique proved successful in curbing code bloat in real use. People who do not use a technique like this have found that replicated code can cost megabytes of code space even in moderate size programs.

*— Bjarne Stroustrup, The Design and Evolution of C++, 1994*

In simple cases templates can be transformed into generics (not causing code bloat) by creating a class getting a parameter derived from a type in compile time and wrapping a template around this class. It is a nice approach for creating generic heap-based containers.

The extra instantiations generated by templates can also cause debuggers to have difficulty working gracefully with templates. For example, setting a debug breakpoint within a template from a source file may either miss setting the breakpoint in the actual instantiation desired or may set a breakpoint in every place the template is instantiated.

Also, because the compiler needs to perform macro-like expansions of templates and generate different instances of them at compile time, the implementation source code for the templated class or function must be available (e.g. included in a header) to the code using it. Templated classes or functions, including much of the Standard Template Library (STL), if not included in header files, cannot be compiled. (This is in contrast to non-templated code, which may be compiled to binary, providing only a declarations header file for code using it.) This may be a disadvantage by exposing the implementing code, which removes some abstractions, and could restrict its use in closed-source projects.

## Templates in D

The D programming language supports templates based in design on C++. Most C++ template idioms will carry over to D without alteration, but D adds some additional functionality:

- Template parameters in D are not restricted to just types and primitive values, but also allow arbitrary compile-time values (such as strings and struct literals), and aliases to arbitrary identifiers, including other templates or template instantiations.

- Template constraints and the static if statement provide an alternative to C++'s substitution failure is not an error (SFINAE) mechanism, similar to C++ concepts.

- The is(...) expression allows speculative instantiation to verify an object's traits at compile time.

- The auto keyword and the typeof expression allow type inference for variable declarations and function return values, which in turn allows "Voldemort types" (types which do not have a global name).

Templates in D use a different syntax as in C++: whereas in C++ template parameters are wrapped in angular brackets (Template<param1, param2>), D uses an exclamation sign and parentheses: Template!(param1, param2). This avoids the C++ parsing difficulties due to ambiguity with comparison operators. If there is only one parameter, the parentheses can be omitted.

Conventionally, D combines the above features to provide compile-time polymorphism using trait-based generic programming. For example, an input range is defined as any type which satisfies the checks performed by isInputRange, which is defined as follows:

```
template isInputRange(R)

{

    enum bool isInputRange = is(typeof(
```

```
    (inout int = 0)

    {

        R r = R.init;      // can define a range object

        if (r.empty) {}    // can test for empty

        r.popFront();      // can invoke popFront()

        auto h = r.front;  // can get the front of the range

    }));

}
```

A function which accepts only input ranges can then use the above template in a template constraint:

```
auto fun(Range)(Range range)

    if (isInputRange!Range)

{

    // ...

}
```

## Code Generation

In addition to template metaprogramming, D also provides several features to enable compile-time code generation:

- The import expression allows reading a file from disk and using its contents as a string expression.

- Compile-time reflection allows enumerating and inspecting declarations and their members during compilation.

- User-defined attributes allow users to attach arbitrary identifiers to declarations, which can then be enumerated using compile-time reflection.

- Compile-Time Function Execution (CTFE) allows a subset of D (restricted to safe operations) to be interpreted during compilation.

- String mixins allow evaluating and compiling the contents of a string expression as D code which becomes part of the program.

Combining the above allows generating code based on existing declarations. For example, D serialization frameworks can enumerate a type's members and generate specialized functions for each serialized type to perform serialization and deserializ ation. User-defined attributes could further indicate serialization rules.

The import expression and compile-time function execution also allow efficiently im plementing domain-specific languages. For example, given a function which takes a string containing an HTML template and returns equivalent D source code, it is possi ble to use it in the following way:

```
// Import the contents of example.htt as a string manifest con-
stant.

enum htmlTemplate = import("example.htt");


// Transpile the HTML template to D code.

enum htmlDCode = htmlTemplateToD(htmlTemplate);


// Paste the contents of htmlDCode as D code.

mixin(htmlDCode);
```

## Genericity in Eiffel

Generic classes have been a part of Eiffel since the original method and language de sign. The foundation publications of Eiffel, use the term *genericity* to describe the cre ation and use of generic classes.

## Basic/Unconstrained Genericity

Generic classes are declared with their class name and a list of one or more *formal ge neric parameters*. In the following code, class LIST has one formal generic parameter G,

```
class

    LIST [G]

            ...

feature    -- Access

    item: G

            -- The item currently pointed to by cursor

        ...
```

```
feature    -- Element change

    put (new_item: G)

            -- Add `new_item' at the end of the list

        ...
```

The formal generic parameters are placeholders for arbitrary class names which will be supplied when a declaration of the generic class is made, as shown in the two *generic derivations* below, where ACCOUNT and DEPOSIT are other class names. ACCOUNT and DEPOSIT are considered *actual generic parameters* as they provide real class names to substitute for G in actual use.

```
    list_of_accounts: LIST [ACCOUNT]

            -- Account list



    list_of_deposits: LIST [DEPOSIT]

            -- Deposit list
```

Within the Eiffel type system, although class LIST [G] is considered a class, it is not considered a type. However, a generic derivation of LIST [G] such as LIST [ACCOUNT] is considered a type.

## Constrained Genericity

For the list class shown above, an actual generic parameter substituting for G can be any other available class. To constrain the set of classes from which valid actual generic parameters can be chosen, a *generic constraint* can be specified. In the declaration of class SORTED_LIST below, the generic constraint dictates that any valid actual generic parameter will be a class which inherits from class COMPARABLE. The generic constraint ensures that elements of a SORTED_LIST can in fact be sorted.

```
class

    SORTED_LIST [G -> COMPARABLE]
```

## Generics in Java

Support for the *generics*, or "containers-of-type-T" was added to the Java programming language in 2004 as part of J2SE 5.0. In Java, generics are only checked at compile time for type correctness. The generic type information is then removed via a process called type erasure, to maintain compatibility with old JVM implementations, making it unavailable at runtime. For example, a List<String> is converted to the raw type List. The compiler inserts type casts to convert the elements to the String type when they are retrieved from the list, reducing performance compared to other implementations such as C++ templates.

## Genericity in .NET [C#, VB.NET]

Generics were added as part of .NET Framework 2.0 in November 2005, based on a research prototype from Microsoft Research started in 1999. Although similar to generics in Java, .NET generics do not apply type erasure, but implement generics as a first class mechanism in the runtime using reification. This design choice provides additional functionality, such as allowing reflection with preservation of generic types, as well as alleviating some of the limitations of erasure (such as being unable to create generic arrays). This also means that there is no performance hit from runtime casts and normally expensive boxing conversions. When primitive and value types are used as generic arguments, they get specialized implementations, allowing for efficient generic collections and methods. As in C++ and Java, nested generic types such as Dictionary<string, List<int>> are valid types, however are advised against for member signatures in code analysis design rules.

.NET allows six varieties of generic type constraints using the where keyword including restricting generic types to be value types, to be classes, to have constructors, and to implement interfaces. Below is an example with an interface constraint:

```
using System;


class Sample

{

    static void Main()

    {

        int[] array = { 0, 1, 2, 3 };

        MakeAtLeast<int>(array, 2); // Change array to { 2, 2,
2, 3 }

        foreach (int i in array)

            Console.WriteLine(i); // Print results.

        Console.ReadKey(true);

    }
```

```
    static void MakeAtLeast<T>(T[] list, T lowest) where T :
IComparable<T>

    {

        for (int i = 0; i < list.Length; i++)

            if (list[i].CompareTo(lowest) < 0)

                list[i] = lowest;

    }

}
```

The MakeAtLeast() method allows operation on arrays, with elements of generic type T. The method's type constraint indicates that the method is applicable to any type T that implements the generic IComparable<T> interface. This ensures a compile time error if the method is called if the type does not support comparison. The interface provides the generic method CompareTo(T).

The above method could also be written without generic types, simply using the non-generic Array type. However, since arrays are contravariant, the casting would not be type safe, and compiler may miss errors that would otherwise be caught while making use of the generic types. In addition, the method would need to access the array items as objects instead, and would require casting to compare two elements. (For value types like types such as int this requires a boxing conversion, although this can be worked around using the Comparer<T> class, as is done in the standard collection classes.)

A notable behavior of static members in a generic .NET class is static member instantiation per run-time type.

```
    //A generic class

    public class GenTest<T>

    {

        //A static variable - will be created for each type on
refraction

        static CountedInstances OnePerType = new CountedInstanc-
es();


        //a data member

        private T mT;
```

```
        //simple constructor
        public GenTest(T pT)
        {
            mT = pT;
        }
    }


    //a class
    public class CountedInstances
    {
        //Static variable - this will be incremented once per
instance
        public static int Counter;

        //simple constructor
        public CountedInstances()
        {
            //increase counter by one during object instantiation
            CountedInstances.Counter++;
        }
    }


//main code entry point
//at the end of execution, CountedInstances.Counter = 2
GenTest<int> g1 = new GenTest<int>(1);
GenTest<int> g11 = new GenTest<int>(11);
GenTest<int> g111 = new GenTest<int>(111);
```

```
GenTest<double> g2 = new GenTest<double>(1.0);
```

## Genericity in Delphi

Delphi's Object Pascal dialect acquired generics in the Delphi 2007 release, initially only with the (now discontinued) .NET compiler before being added to the native code one in the Delphi 2009 release. The semantics and capabilities of Delphi generics are largely modelled on those had by generics in .NET 2.0, though the implementation is by necessity quite different. Here's a more or less direct translation of the first C# example shown above:

```
program Sample;


{$APPTYPE CONSOLE}


uses

  Generics.Defaults; //for IComparer<>


type

  TUtils = class

    class procedure MakeAtLeast<T>(Arr: TArray<T>; const Lowest:
T;

      Comparer: IComparer<T>); overload;

    class procedure MakeAtLeast<T>(Arr: TArray<T>; const Lowest:
T); overload;

  end;


class procedure TUtils.MakeAtLeast<T>(Arr: TArray<T>; const Low-
est: T;

  Comparer: IComparer<T>);

var

  I: Integer;

begin

  if Comparer = nil then Comparer := TComparer<T>.Default;
```

```
   for I := Low(Arr) to High(Arr) do

     if Comparer.Compare(Arr[I], Lowest) < 0 then

       Arr[I] := Lowest;

end;


class procedure TUtils.MakeAtLeast<T>(Arr: TArray<T>; const Low-
est: T);

begin

  MakeAtLeast<T>(Arr, Lowest, nil);

end;


var

  Ints: TArray<Integer>;

  Value: Integer;

begin

  Ints := TArray<Integer>.Create(0, 1, 2, 3);

  TUtils.MakeAtLeast<Integer>(Ints, 2);

  for Value in Ints do

    WriteLn(Value);

  ReadLn;

end.
```

As with C#, methods as well as whole types can have one or more type parameters. In the example, TArray is a generic type (defined by the language) and MakeAtLeast a generic method. The available constraints are very similar to the available constraints in C#: any value type, any class, a specific class or interface, and a class with a parameterless constructor. Multiple constraints act as an additive union.

## Genericity in Free Pascal

Free Pascal implemented generics before Delphi, and with different syntax and semantics. However, work is now underway to implement Delphi generics alongside native FPC ones. This allows Free Pascal programmers to use generics in whatever style they prefer.

**Delphi and Free Pascal example:**

```
// Delphi style
unit A;

{$ifdef fpc}
  {$mode delphi}
{$endif}

interface

type
  TGenericClass<T> = class
    function Foo(const AValue: T): T;
  end;

implementation

function TGenericClass<T>.Foo(const AValue: T): T;
begin
  Result := AValue + AValue;
end;

end.

// Free Pascal's ObjFPC style
```

```
unit B;

{$ifdef fpc}
  {$mode objfpc}
{$endif}

interface

type
  generic TGenericClass<T> = class
    function Foo(const AValue: T): T;
  end;

implementation

function TGenericClass.Foo(const AValue: T): T;
begin
  Result := AValue + AValue;
end;

end.

// example usage, Delphi style
program TestGenDelphi;

{$ifdef fpc}
  {$mode delphi}
```

```
{$endif}


uses

  A,B;


var

  GC1: A.TGenericClass<Integer>;

  GC2: B.TGenericClass<String>;
begin

  GC1 := A.TGenericClass<Integer>.Create;

  GC2 := B.TGenericClass<String>.Create;

  WriteLn(GC1.Foo(100)); // 200

  WriteLn(GC2.Foo('hello')); // hellohello

  GC1.Free;

  GC2.Free;

end.


// example usage, ObjFPC style
program TestGenDelphi;


{$ifdef fpc}

  {$mode objfpc}

{$endif}


uses

  A,B;
```

```
// required in ObjFPC
type
  TAGenericClassInt = specialize A.TGenericClass<Integer>;
  TBGenericClassString = specialize B.TGenericClass<String>;
var
  GC1: TAGenericClassInt;
  GC2: TBGenericClassString;
begin
  GC1 := TAGenericClassInt.Create;
  GC2 := TBGenericClassString.Create;
  WriteLn(GC1.Foo(100)); // 200
  WriteLn(GC2.Foo('hello')); // hellohello
  GC1.Free;
  GC2.Free;
end.
```

## Functional Languages

## Genericity in Haskell

The type class mechanism of Haskell supports generic programming. Six of the pre-defined type classes in Haskell (including Eq, the types that can be compared for equality, and Show, the types whose values can be rendered as strings) have the special property of supporting *derived instances*. This means that a programmer defining a new type can state that this type is to be an instance of one of these special type classes, without providing implementations of the class methods as is usually necessary when declaring class instances. All the necessary methods will be "derived" – that is, constructed automatically – based on the structure of the type. For instance, the following declaration of a type of binary trees states that it is to be an instance of the classes Eq and Show:

```
data BinTree a = Leaf a | Node (BinTree a) a (BinTree a)
       deriving
```

This results in an equality function (==) and a string representation function being automatically defined for any type of the form BinTree T provided that T itself supports those operations.

The support for derived instances of Eq and Show makes their methods == and show generic in a qualitatively different way from parametrically polymorphic functions: these "functions" (more accurately, type-indexed families of functions) can be applied to values of various types, and although they behave differently for every argument type, little work is needed to add support for a new type. Ralf Hinze (2004) has shown that a similar effect can be achieved for user-defined type classes by certain programming techniques. Other researchers have proposed approaches to this and other kinds of genericity in the context of Haskell and extensions to Haskell (discussed below).

## PolyP

PolyP was the first generic programming language extension to Haskell. In PolyP, generic functions are called *polytypic*. The language introduces a special construct in which such polytypic functions can be defined via structural induction over the structure of the pattern functor of a regular datatype. Regular datatypes in PolyP are a subset of Haskell datatypes. A regular datatype t must be of kind $* \to *$, and if $a$ is the formal type argument in the definition, then all recursive calls to $t$ must have the form $t\ a$. These restrictions rule out higher-kinded datatypes as well as nested datatypes, where the recursive calls are of a different form. The flatten function in PolyP is here provided as an example:

```
flatten :: Regular d => d a -> [a]

  flatten = cata fl


  polytypic fl :: f a [a] -> [a]

    case f of

      g+h -> either fl fl

      g*h -> \(x,y) -> fl x ++ fl y

      () -> \x -> []

      Par -> \x -> [x]

      Rec -> \x -> x

      d@g -> concat . flatten . pmap fl

      Con t -> \x -> []


    cata :: Regular d => (FunctorOf d a b -> b) -> d a -> b
```

## Generic Haskell

Generic Haskell is another extension to Haskell, developed at Utrecht University in the Netherlands. The extensions it provides are:

- *Type-indexed values* are defined as a value indexed over the various Haskell type constructors (unit, primitive types, sums, products, and user-defined type constructors). In addition, we can also specify the behaviour of a type-indexed values for a specific constructor using *constructor cases*, and reuse one generic definition in another using *default cases*.

The resulting type-indexed value can be specialised to any type.

- *Kind-indexed types* are types indexed over kinds, defined by giving a case for both * and $k \rightarrow k'$. Instances are obtained by applying the kind-indexed type to a kind.

- Generic definitions can be used by applying them to a type or kind. This is called *generic application*. The result is a type or value, depending on which sort of generic definition is applied.

- *Generic abstraction* enables generic definitions be defined by abstracting a type parameter (of a given kind).

- *Type-indexed types* are types which are indexed over the type constructors. These can be used to give types to more involved generic values. The resulting type-indexed types can be specialised to any type.

As an example, the equality function in Generic Haskell:

```
type Eq {[ * ]} t1 t2 = t1 -> t2 -> Bool

type Eq {[ k -> l ]} t1 t2 = forall u1 u2. Eq {[ k ]} u1 u2
-> Eq {[ l ]} (t1 u1) (t2 u2)


eq {| t :: k |} :: Eq {[ k ]} t t

eq {| Unit |} _ _ = True

eq {| :+: |} eqA eqB (Inl a1) (Inl a2) = eqA a1 a2

eq {| :+: |} eqA eqB (Inr b1) (Inr b2) = eqB b1 b2

eq {| :+: |} eqA eqB _ _ = False

eq {| :*: |} eqA eqB (a1 :*: b1) (a2 :*: b2) = eqA a1 a2 &&
eqB b1 b2

eq {| Int |} = (==)
```

```
eq {| Char |} = (==)
eq {| Bool |} = (==)
```

## Clean

Clean offers generic programming based PolyP and the generic Haskell as supported by the GHC>=6.0. It parametrizes by kind as those but offers overloading.

## Other Languages

The ML family of programming languages support generic programming through parametric polymorphism and generic modules called *functors*. Both Standard ML and OCaml provide functors, which are similar to class templates and to Ada's generic packages. Scheme syntactic abstractions also have a connection to genericity – these are in fact a superset of templating à la C++.

A Verilog module may take one or more parameters, to which their actual values are assigned upon the instantiation of the module. One example is a generic register array where the array width is given via a parameter. Such the array, combined with a generic wire vector, can make a generic buffer or memory module with an arbitrary bit width out of a single module implementation.

VHDL, being derived from Ada, also have generic ability.

# Metaprogramming

Metaprogramming is the art of writing of computer programs with the ability to treat programs as their data. It means that a program could be designed to read, generate, analyse or transform other programs, and even modify itself while running. In some cases, this allows programmers to minimize the number of lines of code to express a solution (hence reducing development time), or it gives programs greater flexibility to efficiently handle new situations without recompilation. One of the types of metaprogramming only involves writing their program is generic programming.

Metaprogramming is used to move the computations from the run-time to compile-time,enable self-adapting code and generate code using compile time computations.

The language in which the metaprogram is written is called the metalanguage. The language of the programs that are manipulated is called the *object language*. The ability of a programming language to be its own metalanguage is called *reflection* or *reflexivity*.

Reflection is a valuable language feature to facilitate metaprogramming. Having the programming language itself as a first-class data type (as in Lisp, Prolog, SNOBOL, or Rebol) is also very useful; this is known as *homoiconicity*. Generic programming invokes a metaprogramming facility within a language, in those languages supporting it.

Metaprogramming usually works in one of three ways. The first way is to expose the internals of the run-time engine to the programming code through application programming interfaces (APIs) like Microsoft IL Emiter. The second approach is dynamic execution of expressions that contain programming commands, often composed from strings, but can also be from other methods using arguments or context, like Javascript. Thus, "programs can write programs." Although both approaches can be used in the same language, most languages tend to lean toward one or the other.

The third way is to step outside the language entirely. General purpose program transformation systems such as compilers, which accept language descriptions and can carry out arbitrary transformations on those languages, are direct implementations of general metaprogramming. This allows metaprogramming to be applied to virtually any target language without regard to whether that target language has any metaprogramming abilities of its own.

## Approaches

### In Statically Typed Functional Languages

- Usage of dependent types allows proving that generated code is never invalid.

### Template Metaprogramming

- C "X Macros"
- C++ Templates

### Staged Meta-Programming

- MetaML
- MetaOCaml

### Macro Systems

- Scheme hygienic macros
- MacroML
- Template Haskell

### IBM/360 Assembler

The IBM/360 and derivatives had powerful assembler macro facilities that were often used to generate complete programs or sections of programs (for different operating systems for instance). Macros provided with CICS transaction processing system had assembler macros that generated COBOL statements as a pre-processing step.

*'Metaclass'*

- Python

- SmallTalk-80

- Ruby

- Objective C

## Examples

A simple example of a metaprogram is this POSIX Shell script, which is an example of generative programming:

```
#!/bin/sh

# metaprogram

echo '#!/bin/sh' >program

for I in $(seq 992)

do

        echo "echo $I" >> program

done

chmod +x program
```

This script (or program) generates a new 993-line program that prints out the numbers 1–992. This is only an illustration of how to use code to write more code; it is not the most efficient way to print out a list of numbers. Nonetheless, a programmer can write and execute this metaprogram in less than a minute, and will have generated exactly 1000 lines of code in that amount of time.

A quine is a special kind of metaprogram that produces its own source code as its output.

Not all metaprogramming involves generative programming. If programs are modifiable at runtime or if incremental compilation is available (such as in C#, Forth, Frink, Groovy, JavaScript, Lisp, Lua, Perl, PHP, Python, REBOL, Ruby, Smalltalk, and Tcl), then techniques can be used to perform metaprogramming without actually generating source code.

Lisp is probably the quintessential language with metaprogramming facilities, both because of its historical precedence and because of the simplicity and power of its metaprogramming. In Lisp metaprogramming, the unquote operator (typically a comma) introduces code that is evaluated at program definition time rather than at run time; Self-evaluating forms and quoting in Lisp. The metaprogramming language is thus identical to the host programming language, and existing Lisp routines can be directly reused for metaprogramming, if desired.

This approach has been implemented in other languages by incorporating an interpreter in the program, which works directly with the program's data. There are implementations of this kind for some common high-level languages, such as RemObjects' Pascal Script for Object Pascal.

One style of metaprogramming is to employ domain-specific languages (DSLs). A fairly common example of using DSLs involves generative metaprogramming: lex and yacc, two tools used to generate lexical analyzers and parsers, let the user describe the language using regular expressions and context-free grammars, and embed the complex algorithms required to efficiently parse the language.

## Challenges of Metaprogramming

We have seen that metaprogramming can help us to give more flexibility and configurability at runtime. However the wrong use of the metaprogramming can result in unwarranted and unexpected errors. Some of the common problems which can occur due to wrong use of metaprogramming are inability of the compiler to identify missing configuration parameters, invalid or incorrect data can result in unknown exception or different results.

## Implementations

- ASF+SDF Meta Environment,

- DMS Software Reengineering Toolkit,

- Joose (JavaScript),

- JetBrains MPS,

- Moose (Perl),

- Nemerle,

- Rascal Metaprogramming Language,

- Stratego/XT,

- Template Haskell.

# Compatibility of C and C++

The C and C++ programming languages are closely related. C++ grew out of C, as it was designed to be source-and-link compatible with C. Due to this, development tools for the two languages (such as IDEs and compilers) are often integrated into a single product, with the programmer able to specify C or C++ as their source language. However, most non-trivial C programs will not compile as C++ code without modification — C is not a subset of C++.

Likewise, C++ introduces many features that are not available in C and in practice almost all code written in C++ is not conforming C code. This article, however, focuses on differences that cause conforming C code to be ill-formed C++ code, or to be conforming/well-formed in both languages, but to behave differently in C and C++.

Bjarne Stroustrup, the creator of C++, has suggested that the incompatibilities between C and C++ should be reduced as much as possible in order to maximize inter-operability between the two languages. Others have argued that since C and C++ are two different languages, compatibility between them is useful but not vital; according to this camp, efforts to reduce incompatibility should not hinder attempts to improve each language in isolation. The official rationale for the 1999 C standard (C99) "endorse[d] the principle of maintaining the largest common subset" between C and C++ "while maintaining a distinction between them and allowing them to evolve separately", and stated that the authors were "content to let C++ be the big and ambitious language."

Several additions of C99 are or were not supported in C++ or conflicted with C++ features, such as variadic macros, compound literals, designated initializers, variable-length arrays, and native complex number types. The long long int datatype and restrict type qualifier defined in C99 were not included in the C++03 standard, but most mainstream compilers such as the GNU Compiler Collection, Microsoft Visual C++, and Intel C++ Compiler provided similar functionality as an extension. The long long datatype along with variadic macros are present in the subsequent C++ standard, C++11. On the other hand, C99 has reduced some other incompatibilities by incorporating C++ features such as // comments and mixed declarations and code.

## Constructs Valid in C but not in C++

- One commonly encountered difference is C being more weakly-typed regarding pointers. For example, C allows a void* pointer to be assigned to any pointer type without a cast, while C++ doesn't; this idiom appears often in C code using malloc memory allocation, or in the passing of context pointers to the pthreads

API and other frameworks involving callbacks. For example, the following is valid in C but not C++:

```
void* ptr;
/* Implicit conversion from void* to int* */
int *i = ptr;
```

or similarly:

```
int *j = malloc(sizeof(int) * 5);      /* Implicit conversion
from void* to int* */
```

- In order to make the code compile as both C and C++, one must use an explicit cast, as follows (with some potentially unpleasant side effects in both languages):

```
void* ptr;
int *i = (int *)ptr;
int *j = (int *)malloc(sizeof(int) * 5);
```

- C++ adds numerous additional keywords to support its new features. This renders C code using those keywords for identifiers invalid in C++. For example:

```
struct template
{
    int new;
    struct template* class;
};
```

is valid C code, but is rejected by a C++ compiler, since the keywords "template", "new" and "class" are reserved.

- C++ compilers prohibit goto or switch from crossing an initialization, as in the following C99 code:

```
void fn(void)
{
    goto flack;
    int i = 1;
    flack:
        ;
}
```

- In C, struct, union, and enum types must be indicated as such whenever the type is referenced. In C++, all declarations of such types carry the typedef implicitly. As a result, C allows declaring type with the same name as a struct, union or enum.

```
enum BOOL {FALSE, TRUE};

typedef int BOOL;
```

- C allows for multiple tentative definition of a single global variable in a single translation unit.

```
int N;

int N = 10;
```

- Enumeration constants (enum values) are always of type int in C, whereas they are distinct types in C++ and may have a size different from that of int. C++11 allows the programmer to use custom integer types for the values of an enum.

- C++ changes some C standard library functions to add additional polymorphic functions with const type qualifiers, e.g. strchr returns char* in C, while C++ acts as if there were two polymorphic functions const char *strchr(const char *) and a char *strchr(char *).

- In both C and C++, one can define nested struct types, but the scope is interpreted differently (in C++, a nested struct is defined only within the scope/ namespace of the outer struct).

- Non-prototype ("K&R"-style) function declarations are not allowed in C++, although they have also been deprecated in C since 1990. Similarly, implicit function declarations (using functions that have not been declared) are not allowed in C++, but have also been deprecated in C since 1999.

- C allows struct, union, and enum types to be declared in function prototypes, whereas C++ does not.

- In C, a function prototype without parameters, e.g. int foo();, implies that the parameters are unspecified. Therefore, it is legal to call such a function with one or more arguments, e.g. foo(42, "hello world"). In contrast, in C++ a function prototype without arguments means that the function takes no arguments, and calling such a function with arguments is ill-formed. In C, the correct way to declare a function that takes no arguments is by using 'void', as in int foo(void);, which is also valid in C++.

- C++ is more strict than C about pointer assignments that discard a const qualifier (e.g. assigning a const int* value to an int* variable): in C++ this is invalid and generates a compiler error (unless an explicit typecast is used), whereas in C this is allowed (although many compilers emit a warning).

- In C++ a const variable must be initialized; in C this is not necessary.

- Complex arithmetic using the float complex and double complex primitive data types was added in the C99 standard, via the _Complex keyword and complex convenience macro. In C++, complex arithmetic can be performed using the complex number class, but the two methods are not code-compatible.

- C99 and C11 added several additional features to C that have not been incorporated into standard C++, such as the restrict keyword, designated initializers, and flexible array members.

- Zero length arrays are valid in C99, but forbidden in ISO C++. The length of bytes field is zero. Such field must be the last field in the struct, struct cannot consist of only zero length array and struct can have only one zero length array.

```c
struct X
{
    int n, m;
    char bytes[];
}
```

- Designated initializers for structs and arrays are valid only in C:

```c
struct X a = {.n = 4, .m = 6};
char s = { = 'a', ='g'};
```

- Array parameter qualifiers in functions.

```c
int foo(int a[const]);
int bar(char s[static 5]);
```

- Variable length arrays. This feature leads to possibly non-coplile time sizeof operator.

```c
void foo(size_t x, int a[*]);  // VLA declaration
void foo(size_t x, int a[x])
{
    printf("%zu\n", sizeof a); // same as sizeof(int*)
    char s[x*2];
    printf("%zu\n", sizeof s); // will print x*2
}
```

## Constructs that Behave Differently in C and C++

There are a few syntactical constructs that are valid in both C and C++, but produce different results in the two languages.

For example, character literals such as 'a' are of type int in C and of type char in C++, which means that sizeof 'a' will generally give different results in the two languages: in C++, it will be 1, while in C it will be sizeof(int). As another consequence of this type difference, in C, 'a' will always be a signed expression, regardless of whether or not char is a signed or unsigned type, whereas for C++ this is compiler implementation specific.

C++ implicitly treats any const global as file scope unless it is explicitly declared extern, unlike C in which extern is the default. Conversely, inline functions in C are of file scope whereas they have external linkage by default in C++.

Several of the other differences from the previous section can also be exploited to create code that compiles in both languages but behaves differently. For example, the following function will return different values in C and C++:

```
extern int T;


int size(void)

{

    struct T {  int i;   int j;   };


    return sizeof(T);
    /* C:    return sizeof(int)
     * C++: return sizeof(struct T)
     */

}
```

This is due to C requiring struct in front of structure tags (and so sizeof(T) refers to the variable), but C++ allowing it to be omitted (and so sizeof(T) refers to the implicit typedef). Beware that the outcome is different when the extern declaration is placed inside the function: then the presence of an identifier with same name in the function scope inhibits the implicit typedef to take effect for C++, and the outcome for C and C++ would be the same. Observe also that the ambiguity in the example above is due to the use of the parenthesis with the sizeof operator. Using sizeof T would expect T to be an expression and not a type, and thus the example would not compile with C++.

Both C99 and C++ have a boolean type bool with constants true and false, but they be-have differently. In C++, bool is a built-in type and a reserved keyword. In C99, a new keyword, _Bool, is introduced as the new boolean type. In many aspects, it behaves much like an unsigned int, but conversions from other integer types or pointers always constrained to 0 and 1. Other than for other unsigned types, and as one would expect for a boolean type, such a conversion is 0 if and only if the expression in question eval-uates to 0 and it is 1 in all other cases. The header stdbool.h provides macros bool, true and false that are defined as _Bool, 1 and 0, respectively.

## Linking C and C++ Code

While C and C++ maintain a large degree of source compatibility, the object files their respective compilers produce can have important differences that manifest themselves when intermixing C and C++ code. Notably:

- C compilers do not name mangle symbols in the way that C++ compilers do.

- Depending on the compiler and architecture, it also may be the case that calling conventions differ between the two languages.

For these reasons, for C++ code to call a C function foo(), the C++ code must prototype foo() with extern "C". Likewise, for C code to call a C++ function bar(), the C++ code for bar() must be declared with extern "C".

A common practice for header files to maintain both C and C++ compatibility is to make its declaration be extern "C" for the scope of the header:

```
/* Header file foo.h */

#ifdef __cplusplus /* If this is a C++ compiler, use C linkage */

extern "C" {

#endif


/* These functions get C linkage */

void foo();


struct bar { /* ... */ };


#ifdef __cplusplus /* If this is a C++ compiler, end C linkage */
```

```
}

#endif
```

Differences between C and C++ linkage and calling conventions can also have subtle implications for code that uses function pointers. Some compilers will produce non-working code if a function pointer declared extern "C" points to a C++ function that is not declared extern "C".

For example, the following code:

```
1 void my_function();

2 extern "C" void foo(void (*fn_ptr)(void));

3

4 void bar()

5 {

6     foo(my_function);

7 }
```

Using Sun Microsystems' C++ compiler, this produces the following warning:

```
$ CC -c test.cc

"test.cc", line 6: Warning (Anachronism): Formal argument fn_
ptr of type

extern "C" void(*)() in call to foo(extern "C" void(*)()) is
being passed

void(*)().
```

This is because my_function() is not declared with C linkage and calling conventions, but is being passed to the C function foo().

# Criticism of C++

C++ is a general-purpose programming language with imperative, object-oriented and generic programming features. Many criticisms have been leveled at the programming language from, among others, prominent software developers like Linus Torvalds, Richard Stallman, and Ken Thompson.

C++ is a multiparadigm programming language with backward compatibility with the programming language C. This article focuses not on C features like pointer arithmetic, operator precedence or preprocessor macros, but on pure C++ features that are often criticized.

## Slow Compile Times

The natural interface between source files in C/C++ are header files. Each time a header file is modified, all source files that include the header file should recompile their code. Header files are slow because of them being textual and context dependent as a consequence of the preprocessor. C only has limited amounts of information in header files, the most important being struct declarations and function prototypes. C++ stores its classes in header files and they are not only exposing their public variables and public functions (like C with its structs and function prototypes) but also their private functions. This forces unnecessary recompiles of all source files that include the header file, each time when changing these private functions. This problem is magnified where the classes are written as templates, forcing all of their code into the slow header files, which is the case with the whole C++ standard library. Large C++ projects can therefore be extremely slow to compile.

One solution for this is to use the Pimpl idiom. By using pointers on the stack to the implementation object on the heap there is a higher chance all object sizes on the stack become equal. This of course comes with the cost of an unnecessary heap allocation for each object. Additionally precompiled headers can be used for header files that are fairly static.

One suggested solution is to use a module system.

## Global Format State of <Iostream>

C++ <iostream> unlike C <stdio.h> relies on a global format state. This fits very poorly together with exceptions, when a function must interrupt the control flow, after an error, but before resetting the global format state. One fix for this is to use Resource Acquisition Is Initialization (RAII) which is implemented in Boost but is not a part of the C++ Standard Library.

The global state of <iostream> uses static constructors which causes overhead. Another source of bad performance is the use of std::endl instead of '\n' when doing output, because of it calling flush as a side effect. C++ <iostream> is by default synchronized with <stdio.h> which can cause performance problems. Shutting it off can improve performance but forces giving up thread safety.

Here follows an example where an exception interrupts the function before std::cout can be restored from hexadecimal to decimal. The error number in the catch statement will be written out in hexadecimal which probably isn't what one wants:

```
#include <iostream>
```

```cpp
#include <vector>


int main() {
    try {
        std::cout << std::hex;

        std::cout << 0xFFFFFFFF << std::endl;

        std::vector<int> vector(0xFFFFFFFFFFFFFFFFL,0); // Ex-
ception

        std::cout << std::dec; // Never reached

    } catch(std::exception &e) {

        std::cout << "Error number: " << 10 << std::endl; // Not
in decimal

    }

    return(EXIT_SUCCESS);

}
```

It is acknowledged even by some members of the C++ standards body that the iostreams interface is an aging interface that needs to be replaced eventually. This design forces the library implementers to adopt solutions that impact performance greatly.

## Heap Allocations in Containers

After the inclusion of the STL in C++, its templated containers were promoted while the traditional C arrays were strongly discouraged. One important feature of containers like std::string and std::vector is them having their memory on the heap instead of on the stack like C arrays. To stop them from allocating on the heap, one would be forced to write a custom allocator, which isn't standard. Heap allocation is slower than stack allocation which makes claims about the classical C++ containers being "just as fast" as C arrays somewhat untrue. They are just as fast to use, but not to construct. One way to solve this problem was to introduce stack allocated containers like boost::array or std::array.

As for strings there is the possibility to use SSO (short string optimization) where only strings exceeding a certain size are allocated on the heap. There is however no standard way in C++ for the user to decide this SSO limit and it remains hard coded and implementation specific.

## Iterators

The philosophy of the Standard Template Library (STL) embedded in the C++ Standard Library is to use generic algorithms in the form of templates using iterators. Iterators are hard to implement efficiently which caused Alexander Stepanov to blame some compiler writers for their initial weak performance. The complex categories of iterators have also been criticized, and ranges have been proposed for the C++ standard library.

One big problem is that iterators often deal with heap allocated data in the C++ containers and becomes invalid if the data is independently moved by the containers. Functions that change the size of the container often invalidate all iterators pointing to it, creating dangerous cases of undefined behavior. Here is an example where the iterators in the for loop get invalidated because of the std::string container changing its size on the heap:

```cpp
#include <iostream>

#include <string>


int main() {

    std::string text = "One\nTwo\nThree\nFour\n";

    // Let's add an '!' where we find newlines

    for(auto i = text.begin(); i != text.end(); ++i) {

        if(*i == '\n') {

            // i =

            text.insert(i,'!')+1;

            // Without updating the iterator this program has

            // undefined behavior and will likely crash

        }

    }


    std::cout << text;

    return(EXIT_SUCCESS);

}
```

## Uniform Initialization Syntax

The C++11 uniform initialization syntax and std::initializer_list share the same syntax which are triggered differently depending on the internal workings of the classes. If there is a std::initializer_list constructor then this is called. Otherwise the normal constructors are called with the uniform initialization syntax. This can be confusing for beginners and experts alike:

```cpp
#include <iostream>

#include <vector>


int main() {

    int integer1{10}; // int

    int integer2(10); // int

    std::vector<int> vector1{10,0}; // std::initializer_list

    std::vector<int> vector2(10,0); // size_t,int


    std::cout << "Will print 10"

    << std::endl << integer1 << std::endl;

    std::cout << "Will print 10"

    << std::endl << integer2 << std::endl;


    std::cout << "Will print 10,0," << std::endl;

    for(auto &i : vector1) std::cout << i << ',';

    std::cout << std::endl;

    std::cout << "Will print 0,0,0,0,0,0,0,0,0,0," << std::endl;

    for(auto &i : vector2) std::cout << i << ',';


    return(EXIT_SUCCESS);

}
```

## Exceptions

There have been concerns that the zero-overhead principle isn't compatible with exceptions. Most modern implementation has a zero performance overhead when exceptions are enabled but not used, but instead has an overhead in exception handling and in binary size due to the need for unroll tables. Many compilers support disabling exceptions from the language to save the binary overhead. Exceptions have also been criticized for being unsafe for state-handling, this safety issue has led to the invention of the RAII idiom, which has proven useful beyond making C++ exceptions safe.

## Strings without Unicode

The C++ Standard Library offers no real support for Unicode. std::basic_string::length will only return the underlying array length which is acceptable when using ASCII or UTF-32 but not when using variable length encodings like UTF-8 or UTF-16. In these encodings the array length has little to do with the string length in code points. There is no support for advanced Unicode concepts like normalization, surrogate pairs, bidi or conversion between encodings.

This will print out the length of two strings with the equal amount of Unicode code points:

```
#include <iostream>

#include <string>

#include <cassert>


int main() {

    // This will print "22 18",

    // UTF-8 prefix just to be explicit

    std::string utf8  = u8"Vår gård på Öland!";

    std::string ascii = u8"Var gard pa Oland!";

    std::cout << utf8.length() << " " << ascii.length() << std::endl;

    assert(utf8.length() == ascii.length()); // Fail!

    return(EXIT_SUCCESS);

}
```

## Verbose Assembly and Code Bloat

For a long time, there have been accusations about C++ generating code bloat.

# Sieve C++ Parallel Programming System

The Sieve C++ Parallel Programming System is a C++ compiler and parallel runtime designed and released by Codeplay that aims to simplify the parallelization of code so that it may run efficiently on multi-processor or multi-core systems. It is an alternative to other well-known parallelisation methods such as OpenMP, the RapidMind Development Platform and Threading Building Blocks (TBB).

## Introduction

Sieve is a C++ compiler that will take a section of serial code, which is annotated with sieve markers, and parallelize it automatically. The programmer wraps code they wish to parallelise inside a lexical scope, which is tagged as 'sieve'. Inside this scope, referred to commonly as a 'sieve block', certain rules apply :

- All side-effects within the sieve block are delayed until the end of the scope.

- Side-effects are defined to be any modifications to data declared outside the sieve block scope.

- Only functions annotated with sieve or immediate can be called.

Delaying side-effects removes many small dependencies which would usually impede automatic parallelization. Reads and writes can be safely reordered by the compiler as to allow better use of various data movement mechanisms, such as Direct Memory Access(DMA). In addition, alias analysis and dataflow analysis can be simplified . The compiler can then split up code within the sieve block much easier, to exploit parallelism.

## Memory Configuration

This separation of scopes also means the Sieve System can be used in non-uniform memory architectures. Multi-core CPUs such as the Cell microprocessor used in the PlayStation 3 are of this type, in which the fast cores have local memories that must be utilized to exploit performance inherent in the system. It is also able to work on shared memory systems, like x86, meaning it can run on various architectures. Sieve blocks can also be nested for systems with a hierarchy of different memories and processing elements.

## Parallelization and Scalability

The sieve compiler can split code within a sieve block into chunks either implicitly or explicitly though a 'splithere' statement. For instance, the following example shows parallelizing a loop:

```
sieve
{
    for (iterator i(0); i<length; ++i)
    {
        R[i] = A[i] * B[i]
        splithere;
    }
}
```

The compiler will implicitly add a splitpoint above the for loop construct body, as an entry point. Similarly one will be added after as an exit point.

In the Sieve System, only local variables to the sieve block scope may have dependencies. However, these dependencies must not cross splitpoints; they will generate compiler warnings. In order to parallelize this loop, a special 'Iterator' class may be used in place of a standard integer looping counter. It is safe for parallelization, and the programmer is free to create new Iterator classes at will . In addition to these Iterator classes, the programmer is free to implement classes called 'Accumulators' which are used to carry out reduction operations.

The way the Iterator classes are implemented opens up various means for scalability. The Sieve Parallel Runtime employs dynamic speculative execution when executing on a target platform. This can yield very good speedups, however running on a single core machine can incur overheads .

## Determinism

Determinism is an unusual feature of the Sieve System. If executing a parallel Sieve program on a multi core machine yields a bug, the bug will not disappear when run on a single core to aid debugging. This has the advantage of eliminating race conditions, one of the most common bugs in concurrent programming. The removal of the need to consider concurrency control structures within a sieve block can speed up development time and results in safer code.

## Supported Systems

The system is designed for hierarchical based systems with homogeneous or heterogeneous CPU cores which have local memories, connected via DMA engines or similar memory transfer models.

Sieve has been shown  successfully operating on multi-core x86 systems, the Ageia PhysX Physics Processing Unit, and the IBM Cell microprocessor. ANSI C is generated if a compiler code generator is not available for a certain target platform. This allows for autoparallelization using existing C compilation toolkits.

```
 3  void offloaded(unsigned char* screenbuf)  {.
 4    float x_incr = (MAX_X - MIN_X)/(float)gWidth;.
 5    float y_incr = (MAX_Y - MIN_Y)/(float)gHeight;.
 6    __offload (( x_incr, y_incr, screenbuf )) {.
 7      for(int j = 0; j < gHeight; ++j ) .
 8        for(int k = 0; k < gWidth; ++k ) .
 9          screenbuf[j*gWidth+k] = mand(k, j, x_incr, y_incr);
10    } .
11  }.
12  .
```

# C++ Standard Library

In the C++ programming language, the C++ Standard Library is a collection of classes and functions, which are written in the core language and part of the C++ ISO Standard itself. The C++ Standard Library provides several generic containers, functions to utilize and manipulate these containers, function objects, generic strings and streams (including interactive and file I/O), support for some language features, and functions for everyday tasks such as finding the square root of a number. The C++ Standard Library also incorporates 18 headers of the ISO C90 C standard library ending with ".h", but their use is deprecated. No other headers in the C++ Standard Library end in ".h". Features of the C++ Standard Library are declared within the std namespace.

The C++ Standard Library is based upon conventions introduced by the Standard Template Library (STL), and has been influenced by research in generic programming and developers of the STL such as Alexander Stepanov and Meng Lee. Although the C++ Standard Library and the STL share many features, neither is a strict superset of the other.

A noteworthy feature of the C++ Standard Library is that it not only specifies the syntax and semantics of generic algorithms, but also places requirements on their performance. These performance requirements often correspond to a well-known algorithm, which is expected but not required to be used. In most cases this requires linear time $O(n)$ or linearithmic time $O(n \log n)$, but in some cases higher bounds are allowed, such as quasilinear time $O(n \log^2 n)$ for stable sort (to allow in-place merge sort). Previously sorting was only required to take $O(n \log n)$ on average, allowing the use of quicksort, which is fast in practice but has poor worst-case performance, but introsort was introduced to allow both fast average performance and optimal worst-case complexity, and as of C++11, sorting is guaranteed to be at worst linearithmic. In other cases requirements remain laxer, such as selection, which is only required to be linear on average (as in quickselect), not requiring worst-case linear as in introselect.

The C++ Standard Library underwent ISO standardization as part of the C++ ISO Standardization effort, and is undergoing further work regarding standardization of expanded functionality.

## Standard Headers

The following files contain the declarations of the C++ Standard Library.

## Containers

<array>

> New in C++11 and TR1. Provides the container class template std::array, a container for a fixed sized array.

<bitset>

> Provides the specialized container class std::bitset, a bit array.

<deque>

> Provides the container class template std::deque, a double-ended queue.

<forward_list>

> New in C++11 and TR1. Provides the container class template std::forward_list, a singly linked list.

<list>

> Provides the container class template std::list, a doubly linked list.

<map>

> Provides the container class templates std::map and std::multimap, sorted associative array and multimap.

<queue>

> Provides the container adapter class std::queue, a single-ended queue, and std::priority_queue, a priority queue.

<set>

> Provides the container class templates std::set and std::multiset, sorted associative containers or sets.

>   Provides the container adapter class std::stack, a stack.

<unordered_map>

>   New in C++11 and TR1. Provides the container class template std::unordered_
    map and std::unordered_multimap, hash tables.

<unordered_set>

>   New in C++11 and TR1. Provides the container class template std::unordered_
    set and std::unordered_multiset.

<vector>

>   Provides the container class template std::vector, a dynamic array.

## General

<algorithm>

>   Provides definitions of many container algorithms.

<chrono>

>   Provides time elements, such as std::chrono::duration, std::chrono::time_
    point, and clocks.

<functional>

>   Provides several function objects, designed for use with the standard algo-
    rithms.

<iterator>

>   Provides classes and templates for working with iterators.

<memory>

>   Provides facilities for memory management in C++, including the class tem-
    plate std::unique_ptr.

<stdexcept>

>   Contains standard exception classes such as std::logic_error and std::runtime_
    error, both derived from std::exception.

New in C++11 and TR1. Provides a class template std::tuple, a tuple.

<utility>

> Provides the template class std::pair, for working with object pairs (two-member tuples), and the namespace std::rel_ops, for easier operator overloading.

## Localization

<locale>

> Defines classes and declares functions that encapsulate and manipulate the information peculiar to a locale.

<codecvt>

> Provides code conversion facets for various character encodings.

## Strings

<string>

> Provides the C++ standard string classes and templates.

<regex>

> New in C++11. Provides utilities for pattern matching strings using regular expressions.

## Streams and Input/Output

<fstream>

> Provides facilities for file-based input and output.

<iomanip>

> Provides facilities to manipulate output formatting, such as the base used when formatting integers and the precision of floating point values.

<ios>

> Provides several types and functions basic to the operation of iostreams.

<iosfwd>

> Provides forward declarations of several I/O-related class templates.

Provides C++ input and output fundamentals.

<istream>

Provides the template class std::istream and other supporting classes for input.

<ostream>

Provides the template class std::ostream and other supporting classes for output.

<sstream>

Provides the template class std::stringstream and other supporting classes for string manipulation.

<streambuf>

Provides reading and writing functionality to/from certain types of character sequences, such as external files or strings.

## Language Support

<exception>

Provides several types and functions related to exception handling, including std::exception, the base class of all exceptions thrown by the Standard Library.

<limits>

Provides the template class std::numeric_limits, used for describing properties of fundamental numeric types.

<new>

Provides operators new and delete and other functions and types composing the fundamentals of C++ memory management.

<typeinfo>

Provides facilities for working with C++ run-time type information.

## Thread Support Library

<thread>

New in C++11. Provide class and namespace for working with threads.

New in C++11. 30.4-1 This section provides mechanisms for mutual exclusion: mutexes, locks, and call once.

<condition_variable>

New in C++11. 30.5-1 Condition variables provide synchronization primitives used to block a thread until notified by some other thread that some condition is met or until a system time is reached.

<future>

New in C++11. 30.6.1-1 Describes components that a C++ program can use to retrieve in one thread the result (value or exception) from a function that has run in the same thread or another thread.

## Numerics Library

Components that C++ programs may use to perform seminumerical operations.

<complex>

The header <complex> defines a class template, and numerous functions for representing and manipulating complex numbers.

<random>

Facility for generating (pseudo-)random numbers.

<valarray>

Defines five class templates (valarray, slice_array, gslice_array, mask_array, and indirect_array), two classes (slice and gslice), and a series of related function templates for representing and manipulating arrays of values.

<numeric>

Generalized numeric operations.

## C Standard Library

Each header from the C Standard Library is included in the C++ Standard Library under a different name, generated by removing the .h, and adding a 'c' at the start; for example, 'time.h' becomes 'ctime'. The only difference between these headers and the traditional C Standard Library headers is that where possible the functions should be placed into the std:: namespace. In ISO C, functions in the standard library are allowed to be implemented by macros, which is not allowed by ISO C++.

# C++ String Handling

The C++ programming language has support for string handling, mostly implemented in its standard library. The language standard specifies several string types, some inherited from C, some newly designed to make use of the language's features, such as templates and the RAII resource management idiom.

Since the initial versions of C++ had only the "low-level" C string handling functionality and conventions, multiple incompatible designs for string handling classes have been designed over the years, and C++ programmers may need to handle multiple conventions in a single application.

## History

The std::string type is the main string datatype in standard C++ since 1998, but it was not always part of C++, and still is not the only standard string type: from C, C++ inherited the convention of using null-terminated strings that are handled by a pointer to their first element, and a library of functions that manipulate such strings. In modern standard C++, a string literal such as "hello" still denotes a NUL-terminated array of characters and std::string has support for converting itself to such an array.

In a 1991 retrospective on the history of C++, its inventor Bjarne Stroustrup called the lack of a standard string type (and some other standard types) in C++ 1.0 the worst mistake he made in its development; "the absence of those led to everybody re-inventing the wheel and to an unnecessary diversity in the most fundamental classes". Over the years, C++ application, library and framework developers produced their own, incompatible string representations, such as the one in AT&T's Standard Components library (the first such implementation, 1983) or the CString type in Microsoft's MFC. While std::string standardized strings, legacy applications still commonly contain such custom string types and libraries may expect C-style strings, making it "virtually impossible" to avoid using multiple string types in C++ programs and requiring programmers to decide on the desired string representation ahead of starting a project.

## Implementation Issues

The various vendors' string types have different implementation strategies and performance characteristics. In particular, some string types use a copy-on-write strategy, where an operation such as:

```
string a = "hello!";

string b = a; // Copy constructor
```

does not actually copy the content of a to b; instead, both strings share their contents and a reference count on the content is incremented. The actual copying is postponed until a mutating operation, such as appending a character to either string, makes the strings' contents differ.

Though std::string no longer uses it, third-party string libraries may still implement copy-on-write strings; Qt's QString is an example.

Also, third-party string implementations may store 16-bit or 32-bit code points instead of bytes, in order to facilitate processing of Unicode text. However, it means that conversion to these types from std::string or from arrays of bytes is a slow and often a lossy operation, dependent on the "locale", and can throw exceptions.

## Standard String Types

The std::string class is the standard representation for a text string since C++98. Compared to C-style strings (NUL-terminated arrays) and the associated standard functions, this class offers several the benefits of automated memory management and a reduced risk of out-of-bounds accesses. The class provides some typical string operations like comparison, concatenation, find and replace, and a function for obtaining substrings. An std::string can be constructed from a C-style string, and a C-style string can also be obtained from one.

The individual units making up the string are of type char, at least (and almost always) 8 bits each. In modern usage these are often not "characters", but parts of a multibyte character encoding such as UTF-8.

The copy-on-write strategy was deliberately allowed by the initial C++ Standard for std::string because it was deemed a useful optimization, and used by nearly all implementations. However, there were mistakes, for instance the operator[] returned a non-const reference, and must be treated as potentially-mutating, even *after* the operator has finished (the caller can legally store the reference and modify the byte after copying the string). This caused some implementations to abandon copy-on-write. Performance problems in multi-threaded applications, due to the locking needed to examine or change the reference count, were soon pointed out. The optimization was finally disallowed in C++11, with the result that even passing a std::string as an argument to a function, viz.

```
void print(std::string s)

{

    std::cout << s;

}
```

must be expected to perform a full copy of the string into newly allocated memory. The common idiom to avoid such copying is to pass by const reference.

```
void print(std::string const &s)

{

    std::cout << s;

}
```

## Example Usage

```
#include <iostream>

#include <string>


int main()

{

    // Literals (double-quoted text) denote C strings, but st-
d::string

    // instances can be initialized from such literals.

    std::string foo = "fighters";

    std::string bar = "stool";


    // The operator != compares string contents for inequality.
This is different

    // from != on char pointers to C strings, where != would
compare the memory

    // addresses of the strings rather than their contents.

    if (foo != bar) {

        std::cout << "The strings are different." << std::endl;

    }


    // Prints "stool fighters". The + operator denotes string
concatenation.

    std::cout << (bar + " " + foo) << std::endl;
```

```
       return 0;

}
```

## Related Classes

std::string is a typedef for a particular instantiation of the std::basic_string template class. Its definition is found in the <string> header:

```
typedef basic_string<char> string;
```

Thus string provides basic_string functionality for strings having elements of type char. There is a similar class std::wstring, which consists of wchar_t, and is most often used to store UTF-16 text on Windows and UTF-32 on most Unix-like platforms. The C++ standard, however, does not impose any interpretation as Unicode code points or code units on these types and does not even guarantee that a wchar_t holds more bits than a char. To resolve some of the incompatibilities resulting from wchar_t's properties, C++11 added two new classes: std::u16string and std::u32string (made up of the new types char16_t and char32_t), which are the given number of bits per code unit on all platforms. C++11 also added new string literals of 16-bit and 32-bit "characters" and syntax for putting Unicode code points into null-terminated (C-style) strings.

A basic_string is guaranteed to be specializable for any type with a char_traits struct to accompany it. As of C++11, only char, wchar_t, char16_t and char32_t specializations are required to be implemented in the standard library; any other types are implementation-defined. Each specialization is also a Standard Library container, and thus the Standard Library algorithms can be applied to the code units in strings.

## Critiques

The design of std::string has held up as an example of monolithic design by Herb Sutter, who reckons that of the 103 member functions on the class in C++98, 71 could have been decoupled without loss of implementation efficiency.

## Functional C++

In the context of the programming language C++, functional refers to a header file that is part of the C++ Standard Library and provides a set of predefined class templates for function objects, including operations for arithmetic, comparisons, and logic. Instances of these class templates are C++ classes that define a function call operator, and the instances of these classes can be called as if they were functions. It is possible to perform very sophisticated operations without writing a new function object, simply by combining predefined function objects and function object adaptors.

The class template std::function provided by C++11 is a general-purpose polymorphic function wrapper. Instances of std::function can store, copy, and invoke any callable target—functions, lambda expressions (expressions defining anonymous functions), bind expressions (instances of function adapters that transform functions to other functions of smaller arity by providing values for some of the arguments), or other function objects.

The algorithms provided by the C++ Standard Library do not require function objects of more than two arguments. Function objects that return Boolean values are an important special case. A unary function whose return type is bool is called a *predicate*, and a binary function whose return type is bool is called a *binary predicate*.

## Adaptable Function Objects

In general, a function object has restrictions on the type of its argument. The type restrictions need not be simple, though: operator() may be overloaded or may be a member template. Similarly, there need be no way for a program to determine what those restrictions are. An adaptable function object, however, does specify what the argument and return types are, and provides nested typedefs so that those types can be named and used in programs. If a type F0 is a model of an adaptable generator, then it must define F0::result_type. Similarly, if F1 is a model of the adaptable unary function, it must define F1::argument_type and F1::result_type, and if F2 is a model of the adaptable binary function, it must define F2::first_argument_type, F2::second_argument_type, and F2::result_type. The C++ Standard Library provides base classes unary_function and binary_function to simplify the definition of adaptable unary functions and adaptable binary functions.

Adaptable function objects are important, because they can be used by function object adaptors: function objects that transform or manipulate other function objects. The C++ Standard Library provides many different function object adaptors, including unary_negate (that returns the logical complement of the value returned by a particular adaptable predicate), and unary_compose and binary_compose, which perform composition of function object.

## Predefined Function Objects

The C++ Standard Library includes in the header file functional many different predefined function objects, including arithmetic operations (plus, minus, multiplies, divides, modulus, and negate), comparisons (equal_to, not_equal_to, greater, less, greater_equal, and less_equal), and logical operations (logical_and, logical_or, and logical_not).

## Examples

Function wrappers can be used to make calls to ordinary functions or to functions objects created by lambda expressions.

```cpp
#include <iostream>
#include <functional>


/* Define a template function */
template <typename T> void printValue(T value)
{
        std::cout << value << std::endl;

}


int main(void)
{
        /* A function wrapper to a function */
        std::function<void (int)> funcA = printValue<int>;
        funcA(2015);


        /* A function wrapper to a function pointer */
        std::function<void (int)> funcB = &printValue<int>;
        funcB(2016);


        /* A function wapper to a lambda function. */
        std::function<void (int)> funcC = [](int value) { std::cout << value << std::endl; };
        funcC(2017);


        /* A function wrapper generated by std::bind().
         * Pass a pre-defined parameter when binding.
         */
        std::function<void (void)> funcD = std::bind(printValue<std::string>, "PI is");
```

```
        funcD();


        /* A function wrapper generated by std::bind().
         * Pass a parameter when calling the function.
         */
        std::function<void (float)> funcE = std::bind(printVal-
ue<float>, std::placeholders::_1);
        funcE(3.14159);
}
```

Function wrappers also can be used to access member variables and member functions of classes.

```
#include <iostream>
#include <functional>


template <typename T> class CAnyData {
public:
        T m_value;
        CAnyData(T value) : m_value { value } {}
        void print(void) { std::cout << m_value << std::endl; }
        void printAfterAdd(T value) { std::cout << (m_value +
value) << std::endl; }
};


int main(void)
{
        /* A function wrapper to a member variable of a class
*/
        CAnyData<int> dataA { 2016 };
        std::function<int (CAnyData<int> &)> funcA = &CAny-
Data<int>::m_value;
```

```
         std::cout << funcA(dataA) << std::endl;

1        CAnyData<float> dataB { 2016.1 };

         std::function<void (CAnyData<float> &)> funcB = &CAny-
Data<float>::print;

         funcB(dataB);


         /* A function wrappter to member function with passing
a parameter */
         std::function<void (CAnyData<float> &, float)> funcC =
&CAnyData<float>::printAfterAdd;

         funcC(dataB, 0.1);


         /* A function wrappter to member function generated by
std::bind */
         std::function<void (float)> funcD = std::bind(&CAny-
Data<float>::printAfterAdd, &dataB, std::placeholders::_1);

         funcD(0.2);

         return 0;

}
```

# Sequence Container C++

In computing, sequence containers refer to a group of container class templates in the standard library of the C++ programming language that implement storage of data elements. Being templates, they can be used to store arbitrary elements, such as integers or custom classes. One common property of all sequential containers is that the elements can be accessed sequentially. Like all other standard library components, they reside in namespace *std*.

The following containers are defined in the current revision of the C++ standard: array, vector, list, forward_list, deque. Each of these containers implements different algorithms for data storage, which means that they have different speed guarantees for different operations:

- Array implements a compile-time non-resizeable array.

- Vector implements an array with fast random access and an ability to automatically resize when appending elements.

- Deque implements a double-ended queue with comparatively fast random access.

- List implements a doubly linked list.

- Forward_list implements a singly linked list.

Since each of the containers needs to be able to copy its elements in order to function properly, the type of the elements must fulfill CopyConstructible and Assignable requirements. For a given container, all elements must belong to the same type. For instance, one cannot store data in the form of both char and int within the same container instance.

## History

Originally, only vector, list, deque were defined. Until the standardization of the C++ language in 1998, they were part of the Standard Template Library, published by SGI.

The array container at first appeared in several books under various names. Later it was incorporated into boost C++ libraries and was proposed into the standard C++ library. The motivation for inclusion of array was that it solves two problems of the C-style array: the lack of STL-like interface and inability to be copied as any other object. It firstly appeared in C++ TR1 and later was incorporated into C++11.

The forward_list container has been added to C++11 as a space-efficient alternative to list when reverse iteration is not needed.

## Properties

Array, vector and deque all support fast random access to the elements. list supports bidirectional iteration, whereas forward_list supports only unidirectional iteration.

Array does not support element insertion or removal. vector supports fast element insertion or removal at the end. Any insertion or removal of an element not at the end of the vector needs elements between the insertion position and the end of the vector to be copied. The iterators to the affected elements are thus invalidated. In fact, any insertion can potentially invalidate all iterators. Also, if the allocated storage in the vector is too small to insert elements, a new array is allocated, all elements are copied or moved to the new array, and the old array is freed. deque, list and forward_list all support fast insertion or removal of elements anywhere in the container. list and forward_list preserves validity of iterators on such operation, whereas deque invalidates all of them.

## Vector

The elements of a vector are stored contiguously. Like all dynamic array implementations, vectors have low memory usage and good locality of reference and data cache utilization. Unlike other STL containers, such as deques and lists, vectors allow the user to denote an initial capacity for the container.

Vectors allow random access; that is, an element of a vector may be referenced in the same manner as elements of arrays (by array indices). Linked-lists and sets, on the other hand, do not support random access or pointer arithmetic.

The vector data structure is able to quickly and easily allocate the necessary memory needed for specific data storage, and it is able to do so in amortized constant time. This is particularly useful for storing data in lists whose length may not be known prior to setting up the list but where removal (other than, perhaps, at the end) is rare. Erasing elements from a vector or even clearing the vector entirely does not necessarily free any of the memory associated with that element.

## Capacity and Reallocation

A typical vector implementation consists, internally, of a pointer to a dynamically allocated array, and possibly data members holding the capacity and size of the vector. The size of the vector refers to the actual number of elements, while the capacity refers to the size of the internal array.

When new elements are inserted, if the new size of the vector becomes larger than its capacity, *reallocation* occurs. This typically causes the vector to allocate a new region of storage, move the previously held elements to the new region of storage, and free the old region.

Because the addresses of the elements change during this process, any references or iterators to elements in the vector become invalidated. Using an invalidated reference causes undefined behaviour.

The reserve() operation may be used to prevent unnecessary reallocations. After a call to reserve(n), the vector's capacity is guaranteed to be at least n.

The vector maintains a certain order of its elements, so that when a new element is inserted at the beginning or in the middle of the vector, subsequent elements are moved backwards in terms of their assignment operator or copy constructor. Consequently, references and iterators to elements after the insertion point become invalidated.

C++ vectors do not support in-place reallocation of memory, by design; i.e., upon reallocation of a vector, the memory it held will always be copied to a new block of memory using its elements' copy constructor, and then released. This is inefficient for cases where the vector holds plain old data and additional contiguous space beyond the held block of memory is available for allocation.

## Specialization for Bool

The Standard Library defines a specialization of the vector template for bool. The description of this specialization indicates that the implementation should pack the elements so that every bool only uses one bit of memory. This is widely considered a mistake. vector<bool> does not meet the requirements for a C++ Standard Library container. For instance, a container<T>::reference must be a true lvalue of type T. This is not the case with vector<bool>::reference, which is a proxy class convertible to bool. Similarly, the vector<bool>::iterator does not yield a bool& when derefer-enced. There is a general consensus among the C++ Standard Committee and the Library Working Group that vector<bool> should be deprecated and subsequently removed from the standard library, while the functionality will be reintroduced un-der a different name.

## List

The list data structure implements a doubly linked list. Data is stored non-contig-uously in memory which allows the list data structure to avoid the reallocation of memory that can be necessary with vectors when new elements are inserted into the list.

The list data structure allocates and deallocates memory as needed; therefore, it does not allocate memory that it is not currently using. Memory is freed when an element is removed from the list.

Lists are efficient when inserting new elements in the list; this is an $O(1)$ operation. No shifting is required like with vectors.

Lists do not have random access ability like vectors ($O(1)$ operation). Accessing a node in a list is an $O(n)$ operation that requires a list traversal to find the node that needs to be accessed.

With small data types (such as ints) the memory overhead is much more significant than that of a vector. Each node takes up sizeof(type) + 2 * sizeof(type*). Pointers are typically one word (usually four bytes under 32-bit operating systems), which means that a list of four byte integers takes up approximately three times as much memory as a vector of integers.

## Deque

deque is a container class template that implements a double-ended queue. It provides similar computational complexity to vector for most operations, with the notable exception that it provides amortized constant-time insertion and removal from both ends of the element sequence. Unlike vector, deque uses discontiguous blocks of memory, and provides no means to control the capacity of the container and the moment of reallocation of memory. Like vector, deque offers support for random access iterators, and insertion and removal of elements invalidates all iterators to the deque.

## Array

array implements a compile-time non-resizeable array. The size is determined at compile-time by a template parameter. By design, the container does not support allocators. Unlike the other standard containers, array does not provide constant-time swap.

## Overview of Functions

The containers are defined in headers named after the names of the containers, e.g. vector is defined in header <vector>. All containers satisfy the requirements of the Container concept, which means they have begin(), end(), size(), max_size(), empty(), and swap() methods.

| | array (C++11) | vector | deque | list | forward_list (C++11) | Description |
|---|---|---|---|---|---|---|
| | (implicit) | (constructor) | (constructor) | (constructor) | (constructor) | Constructs the container from variety of sources |
| | (implicit) | (destructor) | (destructor) | (destructor) | (destructor) | Destructs the container and the contained elements |
| | (implicit) | operator= | operator= | operator= | operator= | Assigns values to the container |
| | N/A | assign | assign | assign | assign | Assigns values to the container |
| | N/A | get_allocator | get_allocator | get_allocator | get_allocator | Returns the allocator used to allocate memory for the elements |
| Element access | at | at | at | N/A | N/A | Accesses specified element with bounds checking. |
| | operator[] | operator[] | operator[] | N/A | N/A | Accesses specified element without bounds checking. |
| | front | front | front | front | front | Accesses the first element |
| | back | back | back | back | N/A | Accesses the last element |
| | data | data | N/A | N/A | N/A | Accesses the underlying array |
| Iterators | begin | begin | begin | begin | begin | Returns an iterator to the beginning of the container |
| | end | end | end | end | end | Returns an iterator to the end of the container |
| | rbegin | rbegin | rbegin | rbegin | N/A | Returns a reverse iterator to the reverse beginning of the container |
| | rend | rend | rend | rend | N/A | Returns a reverse iterator to the reverse end of the container |

| Capacity | | | | | |
|---|---|---|---|---|---|
| empty | empty | empty | empty | empty | Checks whether the container is empty |
| size | size | size | size | N/A | Returns the number of elements in the container. |
| max_size | max_size | max_size | max_size | max_size | Returns the maximum possible number of elements in the container. |
| N/A | reserve | N/A | N/A | N/A | Reserves storage in the container |
| N/A | capacity | N/A | N/A | N/A | Returns the number of elements that can be held in currently allocated storage |
| N/A | shrink_to_fit | shrink_to_fit | N/A | N/A | Reduces memory usage by freeing unused memory (C++11) |
| **Modifiers** | | | | | |
| N/A | clear | clear | clear | clear | Clears the contents |
| N/A | insert | insert | insert | N/A | Inserts elements |
| N/A | emplace | emplace | emplace | N/A | Constructs elements in-place (C++11) |
| N/A | erase | erase | erase | N/A | Erases elements |
| N/A | N/A | push_front | push_front | push_front | Inserts elements to the beginning |
| N/A | N/A | emplace_front | emplace_front | emplace_front | Constructs elements in-place at the beginning (C++11) |
| N/A | N/A | pop_front | pop_front | pop_front | Removes the first element |
| N/A | push_back | push_back | push_back | N/A | Inserts elements to the end |
| N/A | emplace_back | emplace_back | emplace_back | N/A | Constructs elements in-place at the end (C++11) |
| N/A | pop_back | pop_back | pop_back | N/A | Removes the last element |
| N/A | N/A | N/A | N/A | insert_after | Inserts elements after specified position (C++11) |
| N/A | N/A | N/A | N/A | emplace_after | Constructs elements in-place after specified position (C++11) |
| N/A | N/A | N/A | N/A | erase_after | Erases elements in-place after specified position (C++11) |
| N/A | resize | resize | resize | resize | Changes the number of stored elements |
| swap | swap | swap | swap | swap | Swaps the contents with another container of the same type |

There are other operations that are available as a part of the list class and there are algorithms that are part of the C++ STL (Algorithm (C++)) that can be used with the list class.

- Operations:

    o list::merge - Merges two sorted lists.

    o list::splice - Moves elements from another list.

   o   list::remove - Removes elements equal to the given value.

   o   list::remove_if - Removes elements satisfying specific criteria.

   o   list::reverse - Reverses the order of the elements.

   o   list::unique - Removes consecutive duplicate elements.

   o   list::sort - Sorts the element.

 • Modifiers:

   o   array::fill - Fills the array with the given value.

## Usage Example

The following example demonstrates various techniques involving a vector and C++ Standard Library algorithms, notably shuffling, sorting, finding the largest element, and erasing from a vector using the erase-remove idiom.

```cpp
#include <iostream>

#include <vector>

#include <array>

#include <algorithm> // sort, max_element, random_shuffle, re-
move_if, lower_bound

#include <functional> // greater

#include <iterator> //begin, end, cbegin, cend, distance


// used here for convenience, use judiciously in real programs.
using namespace std;

using namespace std::placeholders;


auto main(int, char**)
  -> int
{
  std::array<int,4> arr{ 1, 2, 3, 4 };
```

```cpp
// initialize a vector from an array
vector<int> numbers( cbegin(arr), cend(arr) );


// insert more numbers into the vector
numbers.push_back(5);
numbers.push_back(6);
numbers.push_back(7);
numbers.push_back(8);
// the vector currently holds { 1, 2, 3, 4, 5, 6, 7, 8 }


// randomly shuffle the elements
random_shuffle( begin(numbers), end(numbers) );


// locate the largest element, O(n)
auto largest = max_element( cbegin(numbers), cend(numbers) );


cout << "The largest number is " << *largest << "\n";
cout << "It is located at index " << distance(largest, cbe-
gin(numbers)) << "\n";


// sort the elements
sort( begin(numbers), end(numbers) );


// find the position of the number 5 in the vector
auto five = lower_bound( cbegin(numbers), cend(numbers), 5 );
```

```
cout << "The number 5 is located at index " << distance(five,
cbegin(numbers)) << "\n";


// erase all the elements greater than 4

numbers.erase( remove_if(begin(numbers), end(numbers),

  bind(greater<>{}, _1, 4) ), end(numbers) );


// print all the remaining numbers

for(const auto& element : numbers)

  cout << element << " ";


return 0;
```
}

## The Output will be the Following:

*The largest number is 8.*
*It is located at index 6* (implementation-dependent).
*The number 5 is located at index 4.*
*1 2 3 4.*

## Components of C++ Standard Library

## Algorithm (C++)

In the C++ Standard Library, algorithms are components that perform algorithmic operations on containers and other sequences.

The C++ standard provides some standard algorithms collected in the <algorithm> standard header. A handful of algorithms are also in the <numeric> header. All algorithms are in the std namespace.

### Categories of Algorithms

The algorithms in the C++ Standard Library can be organized into the following categories.

- Non-modifying sequence operations (e.g. find_if, count, search).

- Modifying sequence operations (e.g. replace, remove, reverse).

- Sorting (e.g. sort, stable_sort, partial_sort).

- Binary search (e.g. lower_bound, upper_bound).

- Heap (e.g. make_heap, push_heap).

- Min/max (e.g. min, max).

## Examples

- OutputIterator copy(InputIterator source_begin, InputIterator source_end, OutputIterator destination_begin).

- void fill(ForwardIterator destination_begin, ForwardIterator destination_end, T value).

- InputIterator find(InputIterator begin, InputIterator end, T search_obje (returns an iterator the found object or end, if the object isn't found).

- const T& max(const T& a, const T& b) returns the greater of the two arguments.

- ForwardIterator max_element(ForwardIterator begin, ForwardIterator end) finds the maximum element of a range.

- const T& min(const T& a, const T& b) returns the smaller of the two arguments.

- ForwardIterator min_element(ForwardIterator begin, ForwardIterator end) finds the minimum element of a range.

## Allocator (C++)

In C++ computer programming, allocators are an important component of the C++ Standard Library. The standard library provides several data structures, such as list and set, commonly referred to as containers. A common trait among these containers is their ability to change size during the execution of the program. To achieve this, some form of dynamic memory allocation is usually required. Allocators handle all the requests for allocation and deallocation of memory for a given container. The C++ Standard Library provides general-purpose allocators that are used by default, however, custom allocators may also be supplied by the programmer.

Allocators were invented by Alexander Stepanov as part of the Standard Template Library (STL). They were originally intended as a means to make the library more flexible and independent of the underlying memory model, allowing programmers to utilize custom pointer and reference types with the library. However, in the process of adopting STL into the C++ standard, the C++ standardization committee realized that a complete abstraction of the memory model would incur unacceptable performance penalties. To remedy this, the requirements of allocators were made more restrictive. As a result, the level of customization provided by allocators is more limited than was originally envisioned by Stepanov.

Nevertheless, there are many scenarios where customized allocators are desirable. Some of the most common reasons for writing custom allocators include improving performance of allocations by using memory pools, and encapsulating access to different types of memory, like shared memory or garbage-collected memory. In particular, programs with many frequent allocations of small amounts of memory may benefit greatly from specialized allocators, both in terms of running time and memory footprint.

## Background

Alexander Stepanov and Meng Lee presented the Standard Template Library to the C++ standards committee in March 1994. The library received preliminary approval, although a few issues were raised. In particular, Stepanov was requested to make the library containers independent of the underlying memory model, which led to the creation of allocators. Consequently, all of the STL container interfaces had to be rewritten to accept allocators.

In adapting STL to be included in the C++ Standard Library, Stepanov worked closely with several members of the standards committee, including Andrew Koenig and Bjarne Stroustrup, who observed that custom allocators could potentially be used to implement persistent storage STL containers, which Stepanov at the time considered an "important and interesting insight".

> From the point of view of portability, all the machine-specific things which relate to the notion of address, pointer, and so on, are encapsulated within a tiny, well-understood mechanism.
>
> —Alex Stepanov, designer of the Standard Template Library

The original allocator proposal incorporated some language features that had not yet been accepted by the committee, namely the ability to use template arguments that are themselves templates. Since these features could not be compiled by any existing compiler, there was, according to Stepanov, "an enormous demand on Bjarne [Stroustrup]'s and Andy [Koenig]'s time trying to verify that we were using these non-implemented features correctly." Where the library had previously used pointer and reference types directly, it would now only refer to the types defined by the allocator. Stepanov later described allocators as follows: "A nice feature of STL is that the only place that mentions the machine-related types (...) is encapsulated within roughly 16 lines of code."

While Stepanov had originally intended allocators to completely encapsulate the memory model, the standards committee realized that this approach would lead to unacceptable efficiency degradations. To remedy this, additional wording was added to the allocator requirements. In particular, container implementations may assume that the allocator's type definitions for pointers and related integral types are equivalent to those provided by the default allocator, and that all instances of a given allocator type always compare equal, effectively contradicting the original design goals for allocators and limiting the usefulness of allocators that carry state.

Stepanov later commented that, while allocators "are not such a bad [idea] in theory (...) [u]nfortunately they cannot work in practice". He observed that to make allocators really useful, a change to the core language with regards to references was necessary.

The 2011 revision of the C++ Standard removed the weasel words requiring that allocators of a given type always compare equal and use normal pointers. These changes make stateful allocators much more useful and allow allocators to manage out-of-process shared memory. The current purpose of allocators is to give the programmer control over memory allocation within containers, rather than to adapt the address model of the underlying hardware. In fact, the revised standard eliminated the ability of allocators to represent extensions to the C++ address model, formally (and deliberately) eliminating their original purpose.

## Requirements

Any class that fulfills the *allocator requirements* can be used as an allocator. In particular, a class A capable of allocating memory for an object of type T must provide the types A::pointer, A::const_pointer, A::reference, A::const_reference, and A::value_type for generically declaring objects and references (or pointers) to objects of type T. It should also provide type A::size_type, an unsigned type which can represent the largest size for an object in the allocation model defined by A, and similarly, a signed integral A::difference_type that can represent the difference between any two pointers in the allocation model.

Although a conforming standard library implementation is allowed to assume that the allocator's A::pointer and A::const_pointer are simply typedefs for T* and T const*, library implementors are encouraged to support more general allocators.

An allocator, A, for objects of type T must have a member function with the signature A::pointer A::allocate(size_type n, A<void>::const_pointer hint = 0). This function returns a pointer to the first element of a newly allocated array large enough to contain n objects of type T; only the memory is allocated, and the objects are not constructed. Moreover, an optional pointer argument (that points to an object already allocated by A) can be used as a hint to the implementation about where the new memory should be allocated in order to improve locality. However, the implementation is free to ignore the argument.

The corresponding void A::deallocate(A::pointer p, A::size_type n) member function accepts any pointer that was returned from a previous invocation of the A::allocate member function and the number of elements to deallocate (but not destruct).

The A::max_size() member function returns the largest number of objects of type T that could be expected to be successfully allocated by an invocation of A::allocate; the value returned is typically A::size_type(-1) / sizeof(T). Also, the A::address member function returns an A::pointer denoting the address of an object, given an A::reference.

Object construction and destruction is performed separately from allocation and deallocation. The allocator is required to have two member functions, A::construct and A::destroy, which handles object construction and destruction, respectively. The semantics of the functions should be equivalent to the following:

```
template <typename T>

void A::construct(A::pointer p, A::const_reference t) { new
((void*) p) T(t); }
```

```
template <typename T>

void A::destroy(A::pointer p){ ((T*)p)->~T(); }
```

The above code uses the placement new syntax, and calls the destructor directly.

Allocators should be copy-constructible. An allocator for objects of type T can be constructed from an allocator for objects of type U. If an allocator, A, allocates a region of memory, R, then R can only be deallocated by an allocator that compares equal to A.

Allocators are required to supply a template class member template <typename U> struct A::rebind { typedef A<U> other; };, which enables the possibility of obtaining a related allocator, parameterized in terms of a different type. For example, given an allocator type IntAllocator for objects of type int, a related allocator type for objects of type long could be obtained using IntAllocator::rebind<long>::other.

## Custom Allocators

One of the main reasons for writing a custom allocator is performance. Utilizing a specialized custom allocator may substantially improve the performance or memory usage, or both, of the program. The default allocator uses operator new to allocate memory. This is often implemented as a thin layer around the C heap allocation functions, which are usually optimized for infrequent allocation of large memory blocks. This approach may work well with containers that mostly allocate large chunks of memory, like vector and deque. However, for containers that require frequent allocations of small objects, such as map and list, using the default allocator is generally slow. Other common problems with a malloc-based allocator include poor locality of reference, and excessive memory fragmentation.

A popular approach to improve performance is to create a memory pool-based allocator. Instead of allocating memory every time an item is inserted or removed from a container, a large block of memory (the memory pool) is allocated beforehand, possibly at the startup of the program. The custom allocator will serve individual allocation requests by simply returning a pointer to memory from the pool. Actual deallocation of memory can be deferred until the lifetime of the memory pool ends. An example of memory pool-based allocators can be found in the Boost C++ Libraries.

Another viable use of custom allocators is for debugging memory-related errors. This could be achieved by writing an allocator that allocates extra memory in which it places debugging information. Such an allocator could be used to ensure that memory is allocated and deallocated by the same type of allocator, and also provide limited protection against overruns.

> In short, this paragraph (...) is the Standard's "I have a dream" speech for allocators. Until that dream becomes common reality, programmers concerned about portability will limit themselves to custom allocators with no state
>
> —Scott Meyers, *Effective STL*

The subject of custom allocators has been treated by many C++ experts and authors, including Scott Meyers in *Effective STL* and Andrei Alexandrescu in *Modern C++ Design*. Meyers emphasises that C++98 requires all instances of an allocator to be equivalent, and notes that this in effect forces portable allocators to not have state. Although the C++98 Standard did encourage library implementors to support stateful allocators, Meyers calls the relevant paragraph "a lovely sentiment" that "offers you next to nothing", characterizing the restriction as "draconian".

In The C++ Programming Language, Bjarne Stroustrup, on the other hand, argues that the "apparently [d]raconian restriction against per-object information in allocators is not particularly serious", pointing out that most allocators do not need state, and have better performance without it. He mentions three use cases for custom allocators, namely, memory pool allocators, shared memory allocators, and garbage collected memory allocators. He presents an allocator implementation that uses an internal memory pool for fast allocation and deallocation of small chunks of memory, but notes that such an optimization may already be performed by the allocator provided by the implementation.

## Usage

When instantiating one of the standard containers, the allocator is specified through a template argument, which defaults to std::allocator<T>:

namespace std {

```
  template <class T, class Allocator = allocator<T> > class
vector;
```

`// ...`

Like all C++ class templates, instantiations of standard library containers with different allocator arguments are distinct types. A function expecting an std::vector<int> argument will therefore only accept a vector instantiated with the default allocator.

## Enhancements to Allocators in C++11

The C++11 standard has enhanced the allocator interface to allow "scoped" allocators, so that containers with "nested" memory allocations, such as vector of strings or a map of lists of sets of user-defined types, can ensure that all memory is sourced from the container's allocator.

## Example

```
//__gnu_cxx::new_allocator< typename > Class Template Reference

//https://gcc.gnu.org/onlinedocs/gcc-4.9.0/libstdc++/api/
a00057.html

/**

processor      : 0

vendor_id      : AuthenticAMD

cpu family     : 16

model          : 6

model name     : AMD Athlon(tm) II X2 270 Processor

stepping       : 3

microcode      : 0x10000c8

cpu MHz               : 2000.000

cache size     : 1024 KB

...

processor      : 1

vendor_id      : AuthenticAMD

cpu family     : 16

model          : 6

model name     : AMD Athlon(tm) II X2 270 Processor

stepping       : 3

microcode      : 0x10000c8
```

```
 cpu MHz                 : 800.000

 cache size    : 1024 KB

 ...

 Linux debian 3.14-2-686-pae #1 SMP Debian 3.14.15-2 (2014-08-
09) i686 GNU/Linux

 ...

 gcc (Debian 4.9.1-12) 4.9.1

 Copyright (C) 2014 Free Software Foundation, Inc.

 This is free software; see the source for copying conditions.
There is NO

 warranty; not even for MERCHANTABILITY or FITNESS FOR A PAR-
TICULAR PURPOSE.

 ...

java@debian:~/java/eclipse$ ldd /usr/lib/i386-linux-gnu/libst-
dc++.so.6.0.20

        linux-gate.so.1 (0xb7733000)

        libm.so.6 => /lib/i386-linux-gnu/i686/cmov/libm.so.6
(0xb75da000)

        libc.so.6 => /lib/i386-linux-gnu/i686/cmov/libc.so.6
(0xb742f000)

        /lib/ld-linux.so.2 (0xb7734000)

        libgcc_s.so.1 => /lib/i386-linux-gnu/libgcc_s.so.1
(0xb7411000)


 */
#include <iostream>

using namespace std;

using namespace __gnu_cxx;


class RequiredAllocation

{
```

```cpp
public:

        RequiredAllocation ();

        ~RequiredAllocation ();

        std::basic_string<char> s = "hello world!\n";
};


RequiredAllocation::RequiredAllocation ()
{
        cout << "RequiredAllocation::RequiredAllocation()" <<
endl;
}
RequiredAllocation::~RequiredAllocation ()
{
        cout << "RequiredAllocation::~RequiredAllocation()" <<
endl;
}


void alloc(__gnu_cxx ::new_allocator<RequiredAllocation>* all,
unsigned int size, void* pt, RequiredAllocation* t){
        try
                {
                        all->allocate (size, pt);
                        cout << all->max_size () << endl;
                        for (auto& e : t->s)
                                {
                                        cout << e;
                                }
                }
        catch (std::bad_alloc& e)
```

```
            {
                    cout << e.what () << endl;

            }

}

int
main ()
{

        __gnu_cxx ::new_allocator<RequiredAllocation> *all =

                    new __gnu_cxx ::new_allocator<RequiredAl-
location> ();


        RequiredAllocation t;

        void* pt = &t;


        /**

        * What happens when new can find no store to allocate?
By default, the allocator throws a stan-

        * dard-library bad_alloc exception (for an alternative,
see §11.2.4.1)

        * @C Bjarne Stroustrup  The C++ Programming language

        */

        unsigned int size = 1073741824;

        alloc(all, size, &pt, &t);


        size = 1;

        alloc(all, size, &pt, &t);


        return 0;

}
```

# References

- Verilog by Example, Section The Rest for Reference. Blaine C. Readler, Full Arc Press, 2011. ISBN 978-0-9834973-0-1

- Stroustrup, Bjarne (2009). Programming : principles and practice using C++. Upper Saddle River, NJ: Addison-Wesley. p. 729. ISBN 9780321543721. Retrieved 22 March 2012

- Nicolai M. Josuttis (2000). The C++ Standard Library: A Tutorial and Reference. Addison-Wesley. ISBN 0-201-37926-0

- Scott Meyers (2001). Effective STL: 50 Specific Ways to Improve Your Use of the Standard Template Library. Addison-Wesley. ISBN 0-201-74962-9

- David Vandevoorde and Nicolai M. Josuttis (2002). C++ Templates: The Complete Guide Addison-Wesley Professional. ISBN 0-201-73484-2

- Meredith, Alisdair; Boehm, Hans; Crowl, Lawrence; Dimov, Peter (2008). "Concurrency Modifications to Basic String". ISO/IEC JTC 1/SC 22/WG 21. Retrieved 19 November 2015

- "C++11 Paper N3336". Open Standards. Programming Language C++, Library Working Group 13 Jan 2012. Retrieved 2 Nov 2013

- Becker, Pete. "LWG Issue 1318: N2982 removes previous allocator capabilities (closed in March 2011)". ISO. Retrieved 21 August 2012

- Halpern, Pablo (29 February 2008). "The Scoped Allocator Model (Rev 2)" (PDF). ISO. Retrieved 21 August 2012

- William Ford, William Topp. Data Structures with C++ and STL, Second Edition. Prentice Hall, 2002. ISBN 0-13-085850-1

- Lee, Kent D. (15 December 2008). Programming Languages: An Active Learning Approach. Springer Science & Business Media. pp. 9–10. ISBN 978-0-387-79422-8

- Lämmel, Ralf; Peyton Jones, Simon. "Scrap Your Boilerplate: A Practical Design Pattern for Generic Programming" (PDF). Microsoft. Retrieved 16 October 2016. CS1 maint: Multiple names: authors list (link)

- Alexander Stepanov; Paul McJones (June 19, 2009). Elements of Programming. Addison-Wesley Professional. ISBN 978-0-321-63537-2

# Permissions

We would like to thank the editorial team for lending their expertise to make the book truly unique. They have played a crucial role in the development of this book. Without their invaluable contributions this book wouldn't have been possible. They have made vital efforts to compile up to date information on the varied aspects of this subject to make this book a valuable addition to the collection of many professionals and students.

This book was conceptualized with the vision of imparting up-to-date and integrated information in this field. To ensure the same, a matchless editorial board was set up. Every individual on the board went through rigorous rounds of assessment to prove their worth. After which they invested a large part of their time researching and compiling the most relevant data for our readers.

The editorial board has been involved in producing this book since its inception. They have spent rigorous hours researching and exploring the diverse topics which have resulted in the successful publishing of this book. They have passed on their knowledge of decades through this book. To expedite this challenging task, the publisher supported the team at every step. A small team of assistant editors was also appointed to further simplify the editing procedure and attain best results for the readers.

Apart from the editorial board, the designing team has also invested a significant amount of their time in understanding the subject and creating the most relevant covers. They scrutinized every image to scout for the most suitable representation of the subject and create an appropriate cover for the book.

The publishing team has been an ardent support to the editorial, designing and production team. Their endless efforts to recruit the best for this project, has resulted in the accomplishment of this book. They are a veteran in the field of academics and their pool of knowledge is as vast as their experience in printing. Their expertise and guidance has proved useful at every step. Their uncompromising quality standards have made this book an exceptional effort. Their encouragement from time to time has been an inspiration for everyone.

The publisher and the editorial board hope that this book will prove to be a valuable piece of knowledge for students, practitioners and scholars across the globe.

# Index

Printed in the USA
CPSIA information can be obtained
at www.ICGtesting.com
JSHW052018301024
72690JS00004B/112

9 781639 874620